THE ROMANCE OF WRITING

Also by Keith Gordon Irwin

THE ROMANCE OF CHEMISTRY
THE ROMANCE OF WEIGHTS AND MEASURES

THE ROMANCE OF WRITING

FROM Egyptian Hieroglyphics
TO Modern Letters,
Numbers, and Signs

WRITTEN AND ILLUSTRATED BY

Keith Gordon Irwin

THE VIKING PRESS
New York

THIS BOOK IS DEDICATED

TO the creative artists of long ago who developed *the invention of writing* and so gave man a way of transmitting and preserving a record of his way of life and his great thoughts;

AND TO the gifted people of many lands and many languages who were to modify and perfect *the art of writing,* so that each group might have a way of using and preserving its own literature.

Contents

A Foreword

THE NEWSPAPERS, some time ago, told in excited headlines
of the Egyptian discovery of the solar boat of Cheops, a king
of ancient Egypt. It had been hidden away in a special room
near the base of the Great Pyramid. On its deck was a cabin
to shelter the soul of Cheops. Pottery vessels held food and
drink for his future existence. Plates and eating utensils were
ready for his royal needs. And as the sealed room was opened
there could be noted the faint odor of cedar wood that had
been sealed away for five thousand years.

It made interesting news. But little had been added to the
story of ancient Egypt.

About twenty-five years before, an ancient city had been
unearthed from the seashore sands of the eastern Mediterranean. It had suddenly been deserted thirty-four centuries
earlier. The sands had drifted in. On the work shelves was the
business correspondence of that long-ago time, untouched
and unanswered.

And a few years before this discovery a landslide in the
ruins of another old seaport city of the eastern Mediterranean
had exposed an entrance to the burial rooms of ancient kings,

rooms that had been sealed three thousand years before. And down in the rubbish of the excavated ancient city were old, old writings, cut on stone or molded on metal. The reports of these findings did not make the newspaper headlines. But the things uncovered were more important to a knowledge of the past than many a solar boat might have been. They have meant a rewriting of the early history of the art of writing.

But why—I have asked myself—*limit* the rehandled story to that early phase of the history of writing? There have been so many things about writing that need a newer interpretation, so many additional points of interest that need telling. So the book that started out to give only the origin and development of letters and letter forms has grown in size, finally taking in such strange things as the signs of the music page and the odd marks of the business secretary.

KEITH GORDON IRWIN

CHAPTER I

By the Banks
of the Nile

A Beginning for the Egyptian Story

Some of the early tribes of men left a record of their artistic skills on blocks of stone or canyon walls. Among these were the Egyptians. But most artists of the past did not go beyond their picture-making in building a true writing plan. The Egyptians did. And we may wonder why. Were they more clever or more inventive, or did the times have something to do with it? There are answers now for such questions. The new way of writing started by the Egyptians had its beginning five thousand years ago. Now, an event so ancient might not be expected to leave a record of its happening, but the dry air of the Nile country has preserved and the drifting sands have sealed in what must have been destroyed or lost in another climate. And from these records the scholars have rebuilt the story of the past.

In that long-ago time the delta land near the mouth of the Nile was a mixture of marshland and green pasture. There were many passageways for the water as it went on to the Mediterranean. Most of them were clogged with reeds, and in the reeds great flocks of marsh birds nested. Long-legged herons would walk through the shallow waters; ducks would swim among the tufts of water plants; swift-winged eagles from the hills would come swooping down to pick up an easy meal. But there were no full-sized trees anywhere, either in the delta or in the whole Nile valley.

In ancient times, as today, the Nile never ran dry. And then, as now, a surge of water from the torrential floods of the rainy period in central Africa overflowed the river banks each year. And when the waters subsided, leaving the fields damp and covered with a film of fresh mud, seeds would be planted by the Egyptian farmers. When the seeds started into sudden growth there would be strips of green along the river. Blossom time and seed time would soon follow. And after the harvest the fields would be brown and bare until another season. And, fitting their ways of living to the pattern set by the river, the men and women of the Nile country developed for themselves a simple but pleasant life. An uneventful life? No, not uneventful, for a life that is enjoyed is always full of interesting events. But there were few happenings to get into our history books.

Perhaps a century or so before the year 3000 B.C. the Nile country came under the rule of an able king—Menes, first of the Pharaohs. He had an old stream bed on the west side of the Nile cleared out, using the flow of water for a new crop area. He made his government headquarters near this area. And this place, at first but a campsite, was to become the capital city of Memphis. Almost from the beginning a market-place was set up in the city. And to this market strangers came from far-off places about the Mediterranean with wares to be traded for the grain and linen cloth of Egypt.

Close to the marketplace was a temple, and the priests of the temple supervised the operation of the market. They settled disputes, kept copies of agreements, and acted as bankers. And the keepers of the temple were helpful in other ways. They had learned how to predict with certainty the time of the coming of the Nile floodwaters. They had found that the length of the year was 365¼ days and had used the fact in making a calendar. They had built a plan for measuring distances and land areas, one of the simplest that has ever been invented. They had designed market baskets and jars of standard sizes. They had perfected a balance that could be used in the market, with a simple system of weights to use with it. And they had set up a school to give

A flat-bottomed Nile cargo boat of four thousand years ago, moving south in the evening breeze. The long oars are for steering.

training in the handling of such things; those in charge of the school were giving courses in surveying, bookkeeping, business law, personnel management, architecture, history, and medicine as early as 2500 B.C.

But an important accomplishment of the temple-school was not mentioned in our listing of courses. At some early time a writing plan had been invented, and this manner of writing had been used to keep temple records. As new uses were found for writing, the temple had set up a special branch of its school for the training of scribes in reading, writing, and simple calculations.

Making Words with Pictures

Before the invention of the new writing plan Egypt had used only a primitive way of writing out messages. An example of such a primitive type of handling, as used by an American Indian tribe, is given below. This particular message is now a museum specimen and, beneath it, the museum officials have added an interpretation.

The chief difference between the primitive message-handling of Egypt and that of other peoples was in the skill

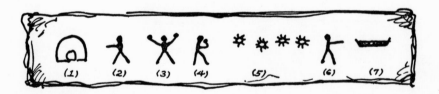

INDIAN MESSAGE: *In the hut* (1)   *nothing* (2)   *to eat* (3)   *and drink* (4)   *We go 4 days* (5)   *in this direction* (6)   *by boat* (7)

of picture-making. In the work of the men of the Nile country it is easy to recognize such things as a snake in the grass, an animal swimming, an eagle, some water birds with long legs, an owl, a goat, a stalk of ripened wheat, a lotus bud; a cup, a bowl, a water-jar; a meandering stream, a sunken garden; a ring, a woman's garment, a sandal; a man and his wife, a honey bee, a bird's egg, a feather; gently flowing water, a loaf of bread, a cake; a man sowing seed, a charcoal fire—and so on down the list of things so common and familiar to Egyptian people. But there were no pictures of great waves beating upon the shore, no horses or camels or tents or gates, no fish or fishing tackle, no baled goods ready for shipping, no monkeys, no ocean boats with brightly colored sails. These would be found later, in the pictures of those who lived in other kingdoms by the sea. To the early Egyptians these things were unknown, and so unpictured.

The Indian message that was shown used pictures to give such *action* ideas as "to eat," "to drink," and "to go." The

Egyptian formal

Egyptian informal

"sky"   "darkness"   "evening"   "night"   "rain"

Egyptians did such things quite fully and cleverly. Two legs
without a body meant "to go." Two eyes without a head
meant "to see"; the eyes with drops below them meant "to
sob." A bee picture followed by three
dashes meant several bees; or it could mean
"honey," the work of many bees.

And from action pictures they went on
to *idea* pictures. A cover, like that for a
mummy case, was their sky picture. To give
the idea of darkness they drew a closed
flower under the roof of the sky. With the
picture of a low sun added, the idea shifted
to evening. A star hung from the sky meant
night. Chinks in the sky with lines running
down meant a shower.

I want to mention at this point something about Egyptian picture-writing that is
puzzling. Why should an artistic people
like the Egyptians have kept on, century
after century, drawing an eagle (for example) in *exactly* the same posture and
with *exactly* the same drawing strokes? And
why is the wife always made to sit still
while her husband does the talking? Even
sandals and dress styles might be expected
to change and not be *exactly* the same for

a thousand years. After putting some more lively and appropriate figures into sketch form, I showed them to an Egyptologist.

"No! No!!" He almost exploded. "You've spoiled it all! You do not have an eagle; you have pictured the idea of *alertness*. You have a *quarrel*, not a family couple. You seem to have drawn a *sore toe*, not a sandal. And your young lady—dressed in outlandish style and not caring about her posture—represents *drunkenness*, not womanhood. *Leave every stroke of those old designs just as they are, or don't draw them at all!*" I had not meant to spoil the meaning.

Now to get back to the new thought that was to transform Egyptian writing. It could have started in the time of Menes. And it might have begun when the Egyptians faced the problem of putting down the names of foreigners. Their handling of such names reminds us of the old game of charades, in which words are acted out. In a charade the leader of one group might say, "Our word is a verb." Then one of his group might sit down and go through the motions of eating. Another might hold up his watch, point to the number 10, and then look hard at the first actor. The word would be "attenuate" (at-ten you-ate). In the Egyptian handling the word parts were pictured, not acted out. To show how their plan worked, let us take English words whose picturing is to present the personal name of ROBERTA. We draw the picture of a man rowing, then add a picture of a bear, then finish with a picture of a big toe. By naming each thing in turn, partially running the words together, we would get ROW-BEAR-TOE. This comes rather close to ROBERTA, the name

Roberta—a picture-charade

wanted. But to make sure that others get the idea, we might add the figure-sketch of a girl, with the understanding that this is an extra, not a part of the name.

It is fun to work out a name in this picture-charade way, and I am adding another example, to be handled in English words; again the sketch at the right is an extra.

——— ———; *a picture-charade*

The Egyptians, using this picture-charade plan, must have found it just as much fun getting the names from their pictures that were strung together. If we knew their words for the objects pictured below we would know that this young lady was known by the Egyptian name of

KAH-ARESA-PUSAREM-KAHERREMT

In Egypt the plan was rather easy to use. Each word-part did not need to match exactly the object-name, though it had to come close to it. And there was a total of about six hundred simple words, with pictures, to work the plan with. In fact, the Egyptians seem to have become quite thrilled with the picture-charade idea and were soon using it for all long words. Their method, of course, was not an alphabet plan such as we have today. Each part was used as a *word*, not as some consonant or vowel sound.

And that, very briefly, is the story of how the people of Egypt made use of a plan that changed pictures into words, and, in doing so, gave a new manner of writing to the world. Eventually their descendants were to forget the old language of the Nile country as they took up the manner of speech of other nations. And when that happened the writing plan of Egypt was doomed. The picture-charade word-parts that once had been deciphered so readily had become meaningless. In a mere century after the death of Cleopatra the inscriptions on temple and palace would mean no more to the Egyptians themselves than they do today to the tourist passing through.

Ready for Dictation

It is easy to get the idea that all Egyptian writing was of the stiff and formal type found on the temple walls, and that all the oldest work was painted or cut on rock surfaces. But writing was being done on papyrus sheets with brushes and watercolor paints back in the days when even the pyramids were new. True, no manuscripts of that long-ago day have been recovered. (The oldest is but 38 centuries old!) But mural pictures on tomb and temple walls that were painted in that far-off time show scribes at work, each scribe with a brush over his ear and another in his hand. Tucked under his armpit is a watercolor palette. And a small jar of river water hangs from an attached cord, ready for use with the paint.

The invention of papyrus sheets for writing purposes was a remarkable one. Other peoples had used tree bark or thin strips of wood. But ancient Egypt was without trees, save the scraggly ones of the delta marshland. In fact, the only substitute for wood, in most cases, was found in the seven-foot, branchless seed-stalk of a common river plant. Being an inventive people, the Egyptians made the seed-stalks do.

To the people of the Nile country the plant having these tall stalks was the *gōmeh*. To the Greeks and Romans it was to be the *papyrus*. In the Bible story of baby Moses it was the *bulrush*. The plant had heavy, bulbous roots that sprawled in the mud at the bottom of shallow parts of the Nile, the leaf

Egyptian scribes

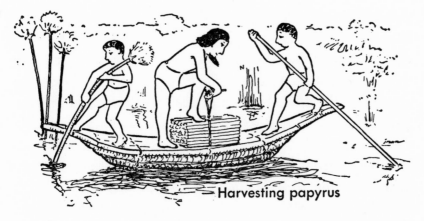

Harvesting papyrus

stalks rising above the surface of the water. Toward the end of the growing season a seven-foot flower stalk would rise from the roots, ending well above the water in tufts of bloom. The blossom parts soon changed to seed. And after seed time was past, the bare stalks, standing tough and tall, made a miniature forest along the riverside. There were many uses for these stalks that could so readily be pulled away from the roots at the close of the season. Some stalks were harvested for a quick-burning fuel. Others, tied into bunches, were long enough and strong enough to make pillars and beams for the simple Egyptian houses. Other bundles of stalks, when smeared with a resinous material, could be fashioned into flat-bottomed boats. Tough bark from the stalks could be woven into baskets and hampers. And the yellowish, fibrous centers, cut into thin slices, were to give the Egyptians their writing material.

It is easily seen that our word "paper" came from the Greek name for the river plant. In fact, there is quite a resemblance between a sheet of the Egyptian writing "paper" and newsprint of today, made from wood fibers. But the methods of manufacture are not alike. The dry papyrus stalks were first cut into 16-inch pieces. After extra drying the pieces were split and the centers cut into thin, flat strips. (Flint knives were used for this, as metal knives had not as yet been produced.) The strips were laid side by side on a flat surface and covered with another layer placed crosswise. Then some cooked vegetable gum would be poured over the mass, the gum filling up the tiny spaces in the pithy centers as well as holding the strips together. Finally the whole sheet, about 12 inches wide by 16 inches long, would be pressed, pounded, and rubbed smooth. The sheets could be made into rolls by pasting several sheets end to end.

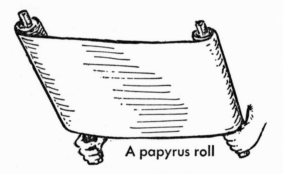

A papyrus roll

Marks were made on the papyrus sheets with a brush. As the material in the sheets was rather soft, the brush strokes were handled lightly, the black and red pigments that were used being thinned with water. The brushes themselves would have seemed to us quite crude. They were prepared from the stalks of river reeds, cut off squarely, and the ends were chewed until only the stubby fibers remained. In a later period of history the reed was given a sloping cut. The point, left chisel-shaped, was then split. In either case, the scribe is always pictured with an extra supply, so the brushes must have been quite brittle or easily dulled.

Special care was needed in handling a long roll. The Egyptian plan was to pass one end of the roll through a split stalk of reed or cane. Then the roll was wrapped about the stalk. Or two stalks might be used, the roll being wound off one and onto the other as the reading continued. For added protection the entire arrangement would be put in a light case for carrying.

That any papyrus writing could have lasted as long as

Formal Egyptian writing is now called hieroglyphics. *In this mural from a king's burial room the picture-charade for his name is set off from the rest with enclosing lines.*

three thousand years is really surprising. In the dry air of
Egypt the sheets could become as brittle as dry leaves. In a
damper climate the parts might separate, the pigments smear,
or the turns of the roll mat together. The oldest of the papyrus
manuscripts in present-day museums is the *Papyrus Prissé*.
It has lasted for at least 38 centuries. On it, as on other
papyrus manuscripts, the design of the eagle is simplified to a
sweeping curve. Other object pictures get a simple handling
also. But the eagle of the brush strokes is still an eagle, and
the picture-charade idea has not been changed at all.

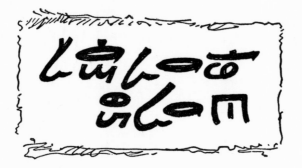

*Egyptian writing on papyrus, in the manner
shown, is now called* hieratics. *The word
shown by the lower line is* SARH. *The symbols
in this line picture an inundated garden, an
eagle, a mouth, and a meander in a stream.*

CHAPTER 2

Libraries
of Clay

Land-of-the-Two-Rivers

The next part of the history of writing takes us to the Babylonian country, a land to the east of Egypt beyond vast deserts. There the Tigris and Euphrates Rivers, coming from the north, run along the edges of a wide, arid plain to join as their waters move out into the Persian Gulf. Today the land-of-the-two-rivers is called Iraq. In ancient times the southern part was the land-of-the-Chaldees.

The great valley plain is largely desolate today; the sluggish waters cross a barren, rainless land. It was that way also when men first came to the valley edge. But there were places where water could be raised from the streams with a pail or tight basket and run out in irrigating rivulets upon the land. Grass and grain could be planted where the water went; cattle could feed on the grass, people on the grain. Later the larger cattle would be harnessed to water wheels that would lift more water to wet more ground to feed more people and raise more cattle. It was not easy work, but the results were good.

Small trading towns were started where streams and highways met. Ur of the Chaldees was one of the early towns. In later centuries Babylon, with the best location of all, was to become the largest of ancient cities. Merchants from the Chaldean country may even have reached the far-away Nile in those days before 2500 B.C. when Egyptian arts were developing so rapidly. And, returning, they may have brought with them a knowledge of the Egyptian calendar, of Egyptian weights and measures, and of the operation of the Egyptian balance. And, without a doubt, they must have brought back also a report on Egyptian writing.

The Chaldeans, like the people of other lands, had originally used only a primitive way of message-writing. With no rock surfaces upon which to chisel or paint, and no trees to use for bark-books, they had turned to clay. That which they found most useful could be baked by a furnace into terracotta tile. Or, merely placed in the sun, it would dry into an almost unbreakable chunk. Any writing made upon such clay was, then, preserved either by baking, if the message was important, or by sun-drying for more common things. The papyrus sheets of Egypt were light and flexible, but they might burn, rot, or drop into dust. The heavy, stiff, and bulky tablets of Chaldea could defy fire and flood. So, as you might guess readily enough, down under the dusty ruins of the ancient cities along the Tigris and Euphrates Rivers are the libraries, the correspondence, and the business records of a long-ago world.

Some day you may wish to look over a sampling of the old business letters of four thousand years ago taken from office files under the mounded dust. Real men, they were—Atidum, Ni Gin, Abu-wakar, Arad-mardu, Ilabras, Ibi, Rammanidinna, and the others whose letters are in those files. You will find them signing notes and contracts, starting ventures in foreign lands, threatening one another with court action, making inquiry about imported garments, reminding a trusted servant to take enough food for the donkeys, offering to rent a shop site for so much down and the rest in easy installments, and so on.

Cuneiform

In connection with the Chaldean story, I have been doing some experimenting. I wanted to find out how easy it was to make drawings on clay. Even on a soft and moist surface, curves are not easily handled. The best one can do, apparently, is to change them into short, straight strokes strung together. (And you spoil the picture by grasping the clay lump too hard or laying your hand accidentally upon the soft surface.) With a stiffer clay the outlines of the curves can best be followed by making jabs with the pencil point or with line strokes by a pencil's wooden edge. But when you do this the resemblance to a curve has probably vanished.

In short, I have decided not to recommend clay tablets for general writing purposes. But the Chaldeans had nothing

Chaldean scribe

else that would do. They had to take clay and like it. They did some experimenting, just as I have done. That is evident. Down *deep* in the ruins of a Chaldean city can be found early examples of their work on clay. Curved lines appear—these could have been made only on a soft, moist surface. *Not so deep* in the ruins are figures made of short, straight lines pieced together—for this a less moist clay must have been used. And *still nearer the surface* the diagrams of figures are of pressed-in wedge marks and indented short strokes made by a special stylus of hard wood or bone. This, the final Chaldean manner of picture-making on clay, is now called *cuneiform*, which means wedge-shaped.

The Chaldean *way of making pictures on clay* was distinctly their own. But the *writing idea* that changed these pictures into words was not. It was the picture-charade idea of the Egyptians. In Chaldean hands, however, the plan followed a new path, for the Chaldean and Egyptian *languages* were vastly different. Egyptian words stressed the consonant sounds; the vowels were merely slipped in to keep the consonants from being run together. And nearly all the six hundred words, with pictures, that were used in Egyptian writing had at least two consonant sounds. How different the Chaldean words were! In them the main stress was upon the

A sample of cuneiform writing

vowel or a combination of a vowel and a single consonant.

To sense the difference, we might take some English words strong on consonants and match them with others strong on vowels. (Bear down on the consonants in pronouncing the first row.)

look	see
dirt	goo
stinger	bee
scare	boo

Not only did the Chaldeans stress vowel sounds, but they had a total of about three hundred simple words, each containing but a single vowel sound. In these three hundred words they had seemingly included every case of a vowel by itself and every consonant joined to a single vowel. This would be quite different from our English words. We do have several, for example, that have the sound of L with a vowel, such as lay, lea, lie, low, all, ell, ill. They had all of these and several additional ones.

The longer words of the Chaldeans were built out of simple syllables threaded together. To give an idea as to how that might be done, we shall use English words. In the left

column are some common words of ours. At the right are
those of almost like meaning, built, in Chaldean style, from
simple syllables.

child	ba-by
don't	no-no
tent	tee-pee
Alaskan	Es-ki-mo

What the Chaldeans really developed, then, was a list of
three hundred simple syllables, and pictures to match them.
Each syllable was only a vowel sound or just a vowel-consonant
combination. Words were made from these syllables, and the
writing was a stringing out of the syllable-pictures.

This use of syllables in writing was so simple in idea that
it came into wide usage along the highways and caravan
routes running out of Babylon. But cuneiform writing never
became universal throughout western Asia. It was not adapted
to a type of language that did not keep to a simple syllable
plan. Thus it was awkward for the Phoenicians. *Aphrodite,*

A dozen of the three hundred Chaldean syllable symbols

the name of one of their goddesses, was written in cuneiform
as if it were spelled A-po-ro-di-ta-ee. The system was also
awkward for the Greeks. Their *Basileus*, as the word for king,
was worked out as Ba-si-le-ĕ-ōō-see.

And it would have been just as awkward for us as it was for
the Phoenicians and Greeks. A syllable plan would, however,
have been just the thing for the languages of the North
American Indians. Their words are built around the singing
tones of the vowels. Perhaps you may have heard of the very
successful syllable-writing plan of Sequoyah, the genius of
the Cherokee tribe. In the early 1800s he constructed, along
entirely logical lines, a manner of writing that used only
eighty-five symbols. The report has it that Cherokee children
could be taught to read in a couple of days. In ten years
virtually every man in the tribe, old or young, was able to read
and write. A newspaper was printed at New Echata in north
Georgia. Many manuscripts in this special writing form are
still in existence. But, unfortunately for the writing plan,
Sequoyah syllables could not handle English words.

*This, the royal seal
of Darius, was used
to press the king's
signature into the
soft clay of a mes-
sage or proclama-
tion. Some seals
were cylindrical in
form. The one pic-
tured was of the
signet-ring type.*

CHAPTER 3

The 'Aleph-Beth

Writing with Phoenician Pictures

We come now to an exciting part of the story of writing, in which the characters are neither Egyptian nor Chaldean. The scene opens about the year 1300 B.C. at Gebal, a seaport on the eastern shore of the Mediterranean Sea. An excellent harbor, large enough for many boats; a place protected from storms that might sweep in from the Mediterranean—that was the setting. Behind the town rose the slopes of the Lebanon Mountains, which were covered at that time by great forests of pine, spruce, and cedar. And from hillside springs an ample quantity of cool water flowed. (Today the forests are gone and the water has slowed to a trickle.)

It was not a young town even then. For a thousand years and more the fishermen of Gebal had spread their nets on the seashore rocks to dry. For a thousand years and more the men of Gebal had cut down the trees and fashioned them into sturdy boats. And for many centuries a fleet of boats sailing each year out of Gebal had carried logs of pine, spruce, and cedar to the Nile country, where wood was needed so badly. For the previous few centuries boats out of Gebal had been

used also in transporting copper from the mines on the island
of Cyprus. This island was to the north of Gebal and a hundred miles from the mainland. And the boats that carried the
metal stopped first at the mainland port of Ugarit. There the
metal was transferred to the caravans that went overland to
Babylon or shifted to boats that went down to Egypt.

Now Gebal was not the only port at the base of the
Lebanons, though it was then the largest, and its location for
that particular time in history was the best. In the thousand
years during which it was growing from a sleepy hamlet into
a bustling seaport there was, we may be sure, a steady need
for men who had a knowledge of the language of Egypt and
who could write reports on papyrus with a brush in Egyptian
style and with Egyptian symbols. Down through the centuries
there must, then, have been many from Gebal who had
studied in Egypt at some temple-school. It could scarcely
have been otherwise. By the time of our story, conditions had
begun to change. Gebal was finding other customers for its
wares besides the people of the Nile country. A way of *writing
the words of Gebal* was now needed, since Egyptian writing
was useful only for the Egyptian trade.

Several attempts toward a writing plan had apparently
been made in the centuries before 1300 B.C., either by the
men of Gebal or by those of the eastern Mediterranean world
who spoke a kindred language. The results of such efforts
appear today as strange marks on pieces of broken pottery
found deep in the dusty ruins of ancient towns; or on spear-
heads engraved with strange symbols; or on cliff walls (as in
Sinai) carrying simple figure-pictures of unknown meaning.
All these were different from one another, and none had been

really successful since it had not lasted. Then, around 1300
B.C., *by a very different approach* from that of Egypt or
Chaldea, the writing problem of Gebal and its neighbors was
solved. The new plan so developed was good—very good.

One has to know something about the languages of these
people to get an idea as to why a good writing plan proved so
hard to build; and why, once invented, it could be used
equally well by the people of several nations at the eastern end
of the Mediterranean. All who lived in the scattered seaport
cities at the base of the Lebanons spoke a common language
—Phoenician, we call it today. Their neighbors beyond the
mountains were the Hebrews, the Moabites, and the Syrians.
Their speech was, perhaps, as much like that of the Phoenicians as Scotch is like English or Danish is like Norwegian. In
all of them the words were made of gruff and guttural sounds
mixed with sharp and explosive ones. These sounds were for
consonants. The vowels, made with an open mouth, scarcely
got a chance and were considered quite unimportant. So
each and every word was to them but *a particular combination
of consonant sounds*. Thus, in Phoenician *n'n* was the sound
combination for *nun* (fish), *m'm* was for *mem* (waters);
and neither the *n'n* nor the *m'm* was used for anything else.
And *g'm'l* meant *gamal* (camel), *m'l'k* was *melek* (royal),
l'm'd was *lamed* (rod), and so on. This method seems strange
to us, for we want both the consonants and the vowels. Here,
for example, are three phrases using our words but giving
only the consonants, as in the Phoenician plan. (The first
word is "America"; you shouldn't need a clue for the rest.)

mrc fr m. Gntlmn prfr blnds. Hr cms th bnd.

Now we come to the main reason why the words of the Phoenicians were so hard to handle in the picture-charade manner of the Egyptians. The longer words were not made from simple object-names stretched on one after the other as was the case in Egypt and Chaldea. They were developed instead by adding extra consonant sounds. We do about the same thing. We can make up long words like "busybody" and "ragamuffin," in which the parts are words in themselves. But more often the added parts are not words, as in changing "judge" to "judgment," "love" to lovely," "swing" to swinging." You cannot picture "ment," or "ly," or "ing"; they are not objects. So the regular picture-charade plan just would not work with the longer Phoenician words—nor with ours.

Around the year 1300 B.C. a *modified* picture-charade arrangement was worked out by the Phoenicians. Who thought of it first we shall never know. Whether it appeared in the beginning in a crude form we cannot as yet be sure. But we do know that the plan was used in Gebal 32 centuries ago, that it was fully perfected then. We know too that it reached the Hebrews, Moabites, and Syrians a few centuries later.

The new arrangement may seem to us quite simple. I have a firm belief, however, that the people of that ancient world found it anything but easy. And I also feel sure that only a vigorous temple-school, such as that of the Temple of Aphrodite in Gebal, could have put the plan into successful use. Here is the way the modified picture-charade plan of the Phoenicians worked. The picture of a fish was to be used

not for the word *nun* (fish) but only for the first consonant
sound in the word. The whole word would be shown by two
fish pictures in a row—one for each N sound. (This sounds
somewhat crazy. *Nun* means *fish* and should need but one
fish picture. Two fish pictures would seem to mean two fishes.
Instead, they meant only one fish.) Again, a picture of waves
was to be used not for the word *mem* (waters) but for the
M sound only. To write out the full word needed two pictures
of waves, just alike. For *gamal* they put down the picture of a
camel (for the G sound), then the picture of waves (for the
M sound), and finally a picture of a rod (for the L sound).
They spelled the pictures out as *gamal-mem-lamed*, or *camel-
waters-rod*, as we would say. (Just the first picture would seemingly have been enough; it showed a camel.)

Perhaps I am merely confusing you, so I shall try out their
idea with our own pictures and with English words. (We
shall need some clues; the Phoenicians would not have.)

PICTURE-CHARADE SYMBOLS	NAMES OF SYMBOLS	CONSO-NANTS	CLUE	WORD
	Boy-Dog	B D	Furni-ture	Bed
	Rabbit-Goat	R G	Scrap of cloth	_____
	Pot-Top	P T	Tame animal	_____
	_____	_____	To talk and talk	_____
	_____	_____	To bathe lightly	_____

The details of the Phoenician plan were worked out thoroughly. Each and every consonant sound in the language was first determined. There were twenty-two of them. Next an object was selected for each sound that had that particular sound at the beginning of its name. There were twenty-two of these, all of them common at that time. Then a simple picture of each object was designed for brush handling on papyrus. It was necessary that the designs be definitely unlike, to avoid confusion. Finally the names and designs were made into a list for easy memorizing.

The list of "letters" started off with five objects common about the home or on the highway. Further on in the series there were six "letters" representing such body parts as the hand, hollow of the palm, eye, head, mouth, and molar tooth. There was one showing a monkey. The rest of the list was made up of pictures of waves, a fish, a fishing pole, a marked bale of goods, a balance, a temple pillar, a spool of yarn, and a rod of authority carried by a teacher or overseer.

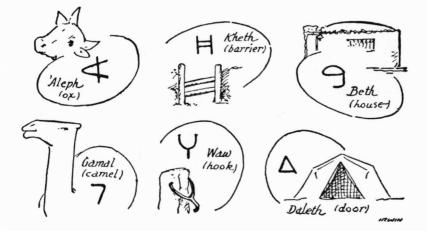

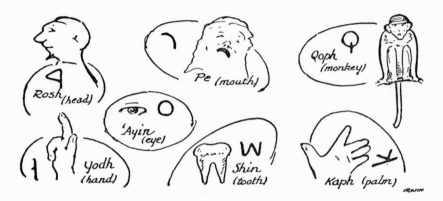

The meanings I have put down for the Phoenician objects are from the writings of the archaeologist Maurice Dunand, who supervised the excavations of ancient Gebal. But for all his great knowledge, Dunand has suggested no translation for the simple word *hĕ*, for the fifth letter. He states that there is no record in later centuries of an object of that name. The picture looks like a comb for carding wool—which is my opinion, not that of Dunand. But anyway, words do get lost. How about some that were common enough in Colonial times? Who knows today that a *clew* meant a ball of yarn?

There may be a difference of opinion as to whether the Phoenician letter symbols were adequate as pictures. It is my feeling that a very good job was done. I find myself, however, wondering about the camel's picture. It seems to be just a line for the head and another for the neck; the rest has to be imagined. But perhaps these are the important lines.

Phoenician

'Aleph	Beth	Gamal	Daleth	Hé	Wuw	Zayin	Kheth	Teth	Yodh	Kaph
[breathing]	b	g	d	h	w	z	kh	between t th	y(cons)	k

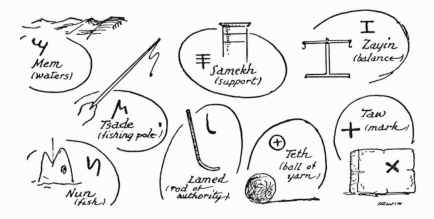

And the fish is just a head. I would have preferred a tail and fins also; my symbol would have been too complex. The ox-head looks overly twisted, as though the animal were trying to look over a high fence; maybe that was intentional. But, all in all, the results are excellent.

You may have wondered about the use of an apostrophe in the name of the ox-head letter. This is for a consonant, starting off the word, that people like ourselves cannot pronounce. The inverted high-comma in their letter that pictures an eye is for a gruff consonant that we also cannot use. A few of the other sounds are none too easy, but the rest of the Phoenician list are for letter sounds that agree with our own. And if we call the Phoenician list the *'aleph-beth*, from their first two letters, it would be but anticipating our name of *alphabet*.

'aleph-beth

Lamed	Mem	Nun	Samekh	'Ayin	Pe	Tsade	Qoph	Rosh	Shin	Taw
l	५	५	丰	O	⌐	⅄	Q	⅂	W	+
l	m	n	s (ks)	[guttural]	p	ts	emphatic-k	r	sh	t

From Mesha to Tyre

There are some interesting features of the Phoenician tale that have not yet been told. We may list, in particular, the Mesha Stone, the sarcophagus of King Akhiram, the buried town of Ugarit that had been lost for three thousand years, and the Phoenician citadel and harbor-port built on some rocks in the Mediterranean. The part about the Mesha Stone comes first.

About a century ago a European traveler, climbing the hill road east of the Jordan River, on beyond ancient Jericho in Palestine, chanced to notice the top of a slab of black rock that was largely hidden by drifting earth. Brushing away the surface material, he uncovered one side of a memorial stone carrying a written record in ancient Phoenician letter symbols. Unable to lift the stone, he got some artist's molding material and made a careful cast of the writing. This was fortunate. The Arabs, sensing that the stone had money value, were to break it up before he got back and sell the pieces separately. Not all the parts were ever recovered, but the rest could be supplied from the cast he had made.

The memorial stone had been buried for well over two thousand years, for it carried a report to the Moabites of 875 B.C. about the exploits of Mesha, their king. On it the words were separated by dots, the sentences by vertical lines. The writing ran from right to left in Phoenician style. The exploits referred to upon the stone got into the Bible record also (II Kings, 3:4–5), which is the reason why the date of the stone is so certain. The Bible account says that Mesha was a

sheepmaster—he and the men of Moab had great flocks of
sheep. The animals would, of course, be scattered in small
flocks over the hill country and moved from one pasture to
another as the season advanced. Winter rains were not always plentiful in Moab, and the sizes of the flocks may have
varied with the years. Shortly before Mesha's day marauders
from across the Jordan had raided the hill country and carried
away the sheep or demanded tribute from the Moab king.

The Mesha Stone

Two lines

Bible

4 ¶ And Mesha king of Moab was a
sheepmaster, and rendered unto the king
of Israel an hundred thousand lambs,
and an hundred thousand rams, with the
wool.
5 But it came to pass, when Ahab was
dead, that the king of Moab rebelled
against the king of Israel.

The Bible account gives the yearly tribute as 100,000 lambs and 100,000 rams with the wool. (The figures seem almost impossibly large!) When Mesha came to the throne he upset the tactics of the raiders. He armed his men, built the town walls higher, then refused to pay tribute. He was finally able to destroy those sent against him. It is the record of the military events and the final victory that is engraved on the Mesha Stone.

Since this first discovery other memorial stones have been found, but farther to the north. Other things have also been found that carry writings in Phoenician symbols. A broken bronze bowl was recovered from the seashore sands of Cyprus; writings were found on a rock-cut waterway near Jerusalem; an engraved spearhead was found in Palestine ruins—and so on. Some of this writing could be dated as far back as 1000 B.C.

There was new excitement among archaeologists and historians in the year 1922 when a landslide at the edge of the ruined citadel of ancient Gebal left open an entrance to the burial rooms of the ancient kings. On a large sarcophagus of Akhiram, one of the kings, the inscription was in Phoenician letters. Excavations were soon begun in earnest all over the old ruins. Down in the accumulated rubbish around the citadel several examples of Phoenician writing were found that were older than that on the sarcophagus. One was on the citadel rock itself, others on stone or metal that had become broken or discarded. The oldest could be roughly dated at about 1300 B.C.

Going still deeper, the excavators found elaborate writing on bronze and stone that was not in Phoenician letters. It

ꞏℒ૭ꞇⱯℒꞩ'Ꞁ૧ꓭⱯꞩꞩꞌℒ◌Ꝺꓕ

TBOL·BN AHRM, MLK GBL

ben Ahiram, melek Gebal

son of Ahiram king of Gebal —

The top row of letter symbols is a portion of a sarcophagus inscription, written from right to left. The second row shows the same letters in our way of writing. The Phoenicians did not put in the vowels. The third row gives the words with the vowels put in. The meaning is given in the lowest line.

looked somewhat like Egyptian work but wasn't. The able French scholar Edouard Dhorme has partially deciphered the wording. He is certain that the "pseudo-hieroglyphic" handling, as he calls it, represents Phoenician words treated in the picture-charade manner of the Egyptians. He thinks the work on the main bronze plate was done by a Gebal temple-school about the year 1375 B.C. Since some pseudo-hieroglyphic symbols are found scratched on the oldest of the samples of alphabet writing in the Gebal ruins, Dunand concluded that the older writing method was discarded shortly after the alphabet plan was invented. And this evidence would put the date of the new invention about 1300 B.C., or a little before.

There was another burst of excitement in the archaeological world in 1929, when a different group of excavators dug into the mounded ruins of a seaport city that had been buried under the shore sands for three thousand years. This, the very ancient city of Ugarit, was north of the Phoenician cities and a hundred miles directly east of the island of Cyprus. Boats carrying copper from Cyprus would steer for its plainly seen, well-protected harbor—features that were enormously important at a time when only dire necessity would cause a sea-captain to sail out of sight of land or venture out at night. At Ugarit the metal would be transferred to caravans going north into the Hittite country or, through Syria, on to busy, far-away Babylon. But as seamen became bolder the sea routes were changed to run directly from Cyprus to the northern Phoenician cities, and the caravan route to Babylon was shifted so as to start near Gebal. Almost overnight the old

Three examples of alphabetic writing, oldest in the world, found in the ruins of Phoenician Gebal.

marketplace of Ugarit was deserted by merchants and seamen. Only the caravan route to the north was left, and its
importance soon dwindled away. So Ugarit just closed up
its shops. Not a skeleton, for example, was to be found in
the empty corridors of the room of the scribes when the excavators dug the sand away. The clerks and scribes had apparently taken the last boat out or joined the last caravan.

And this is what the excavators found. In the room of
the scribes the library manuscripts and practice lessons were
still spread out, the correspondence still piled up, the equipment still intact. Clay tablets were used throughout the room,
showing the influence of the Babylon traders upon the business of Ugarit. Eight kinds of writing were in evidence, but
the alphabet writing of Gebal was missing. One of the eight
was new to the scholars who investigated the discoveries. It
was the one in most abundant use, so must have been that of
the Syrian merchants of the city. It was made on clay with
a cuneiform stylus, but the symbols had no exact likeness to
those previously known. A total of but thirty-two symbols had
been used; not three hundred, as in the Chaldean writing.

Photographic copies of the "pseudo-cuneiform" type of
writing appeared in due time in an archaeological journal.
Three scholars, working independently and in different world
locations, almost immediately came up with the same de-
cipherment. All of them concluded that the plan used was
an alphabetic one with symbols used for sounds, not words.
There seemed to be an extra supply of such symbols. Each
scholar suggested that some of the extras were for vowels,
others for special guttural consonants in use among the
Syrians but missing from the words of the Phoenicians,

Hebrews, and Moabites. Not a single one of the scholars could discover in the marks punched out by the stylus any resemblance to a pictured object. The time of the abandonment of Ugarit has been set as between 1400 B.C. and 1360 B.C. This has been decided from the style of Babylonian wording used in the formal trade treaties found in the palace library. It can be supposed, then, that the Syrian manner of alphabet writing came before the Phoenician plan was worked out. The part played by the men of Gebal would have been in perfecting the scheme, not in creating it.

Our story now shifts to Tyre, youngest of the Phoenician cities of ancient times and destined to be the greatest of them all. Near its location there had long been a small and quite unimportant trading post on a pinched-off bit of seacoast. Near it a rocky spur of the Lebanons ran down to the sea. To the Egyptians, this place was Usu. The spur itself sank from sight half a mile offshore, leaving above the water a

Phoenician scribe

rough and rocky island flanked by a few smaller islands. About the year 1100 B.C., or shortly after, a boldly executed project changed these outlying rocks into the finest harbor and the strongest fortress along the eastern Mediterranean. A wall of fashioned stone was first built on the seaward side, binding the three main islands together. Behind this breakwater the sand scooped out of the nearby sea was used to fill in the spaces between the islands, leaving two deep, well-protected harbors where the sand had been. Stone-built docks and broad landing places completed the project. An abundance of cool spring water was available on the mainland across from the island.

This citadel-and-harbor was named Tyre—"the rock." Within a century it was a city also, with the homes of merchants rising tier upon tier along the rocky slopes. At the rock pinnacle were a temple, a royal palace, and a piazza for national assemblies. Warehouses had been built along the docks, and others upon the mainland. The harbor of nearby Sidon had also been improved, and to the two cities there came by sealane and by caravan the goods of an ancient world to be bought and sold. There were silver and iron, tin and lead from Tarshish; slaves, copper, and bronze from Tubal and Mesheck; ivory and ebony and gay things for the chariots, from far off Dedan; spices, precious stones, and gold from Sheba; fine linen and embroidered work from Aram; horses and mules from Togarmah; carved ivory from the Isles of Chittim; lambs, rams, and goats from Kedar and Arabia; cedar chests filled with rich and beautiful linens from Haran and Asshur. And from places nearer there were wine and wool from Damascus; honey, wheat, and olive oil from Israel.

Some of these places cannot be found in a modern atlas. But the old Hebrew prophet Ezekiel must have known where they were; it was he who wrote these things down.

The Phoenician shops were famous at that time for their own manufactured products. Their workers were skilled in handling wood and ivory and alabaster, in the cutting and polishing of precious stones. Their glass workers made little vials to be filled with rare perfumes; their potters fashioned blue plates and bowls and vases. Even more widely famed were those who gathered tiny sea mollusks and knew the chemical secret of getting from them the prized scarlet and

Boats of Tyre

royal-purple dyes that only royalty and high officials might use. Not all who lived and worked in those shops were Phoenicians in origin. But the language of the workers, the language of the merchants, and the language of the seamen was always Phoenician. And the manner of writing was always of the 'aleph-beth kind learned in the temple-schools of Phoenicia.

CHAPTER 4

Tales of the Greeks

Kadmus Superintends a Job

We are ready now for the Greek story. But we shall not start it with the love-life of Helen of Troy or the tale of the Trojan horse, as the Greeks themselves might have done. The Greeks picked up alphabet writing from the Phoenicians. That statement may make the matter appear neither strange nor important. Actually the situation was startlingly strange and tremendously important. The Greeks were Europeans, and their European type of language was *very* different from that of the Phoenicians. Their vowels had a more singing tone, the lips-tongue-teeth sounds of the consonants were more lightly treated. The word-building ways were different also. And the vocabularies of the two nations were as unlike as the peoples themselves.

The Greeks had not always lived in the land of Hellas, as they called their Greek peninsula. In the early dawn of history they were farther to the north, a wild, semi-barbarous people. Some change in climate around 1300 B.C. is believed to have started the wild herdmen down into Hellas in a desperate search for new homes. By 1200 B.C. they had taken over the

Greek race in armor

mainland and, after crossing the narrow water gap, had over-
run the island of Crete. A second wave of Greek invaders
came down from the north about a century later. They had
boats and followed the seacoast, taking over the islands and
nearby shores both of Hellas and of Asia across from it.

The Greeks had met the Phoenicians in the Black Sea area,
where small Phoenician boats came swarming through the
Dardanelles each summer, loaded with goods for trade. Later
the captains of these boats may have regretted their large
sale of knives and swords, for the vigorous Greeks, now well
armed, turned to piracy. The Phoenicians sought security by
running their boats in convoys. The Greeks countered by
building forts and making raids on the merchant boats. Troy,
near the narrow passageway to the Black Sea, was a nest of
primitive robber-barons. Athens, farther south, began as a
robber outpost, Corinth as a site of pirates.

By 800 B.C. the Phoenicians had given up the Black Sea

trade as well as that around Hellas and had shifted to the western end of the Mediterranean. At about this time the Greeks learned to write with an alphabet. Greek legend has given credit for this to Kadmus, a Phoenician prince who had come to central Hellas in search of a sister who had been kidnaped, and who stayed on to found a city. The legend sounds reasonable. The task of adjusting the Phoenician way of writing to Greek uses was no easy matter. It demanded the thoughtful efforts of one familiar with both the Phoenician and the Greek manner of speech. Kadmus of central Hellas would seem to have had those qualifications. (The scholars of today, ignoring some of the details of the old legend, have tended to place *their* Kadmus on the island of Thera, near Crete, where so many early Greek inscriptions have been found.)

It is not hard to imagine the kind of sales talk Kadmus might have used with his Greek friends who wanted to learn to write. Putting down in order the twenty-two Phoenician letter symbols, he could have pointed out that each had a name. "This is *'aleph*, this *beth*, this *gamal*, and so on. It is the first sound in the name that counts—just the first sound. Words are made from sounds like this, strung together. You put down these marks in the order that the sounds appear in any word. Another person can then look at the marks and tell what the word is. You have made the marks speak for you."

To Kadmus, a Phoenician, all the twenty-two letter names were easy to pronounce. But to the Greeks gathered about him only half of the list was easy, for these letter names be-

A Greek

gan with consonant sounds familiar to the Greeks. A few
were fairly difficult; the rest were impossible. Here are the
two sets of names, Phoenician and Greek, for the eleven that
were easy for the Greeks to handle:

beth	gamal	daleth	zayin	kaph
beta	gamma	delta	zeta	kappa

lamed	mem	nun	pe	rosh	taw
lambda	mu	nu	pi	rho	tau

Two letter names of the Phoenicians were a little difficult
for the Greeks: *teth* and *qoph*. The Phoenicians gave to the
first a "hard-T" sound about like our T in "ting." The tongue
tip is up against the roof of the mouth in sounding it. The
Greeks changed the name to *theta*, with the first sound

produced by the tongue against the back of the teeth. (In pronouncing the Greek word, *don't* put your tongue past the teeth as for our word "think." That would be right for neither the Phoenician nor the Greek sound.) The first sound of *qoph* is about that of our K in "Look!" It is emphatic. (How odd the Q seems without a U to follow it!) The Greeks called it *koppa;* but they had no real use for the letter and soon dropped it.

That left nine. These gave the real trouble.

Three were for the hissing and hushing sounds so different among the various languages. In the Phoenician list were: *samekh,* with a sharp-S sound about like our S in "Silly!"; *tsade* for the TS sound that we put into "fits"; and *shin* for the SH sound that we have no trouble with but the Greeks did. And not one of the three was for soft S which we and the Greeks use so much. The Greeks were confused. What should they do with the three Phoenician symbols? One of them would have to be assigned to the soft-S sound; but which one? One group of Greeks chose the *tsade* and renamed it *san;* another group took *shin* and called it *sigma.* That left the *samekh.* One group renamed it *xi* and used it for the sound we give to X in "ax." The other group dropped it.

That left six. Four of these were the *unpronounceables.*

The odd thing about the whole matter was that these four did not give the Greeks any trouble. They could not pronounce the first sound so they simply left it off. The second sound was a vowel. They kept *it.* In that way the Greeks got four vowel-sound letters that were not in the Phoenician list as vowels.

'aleph (with its unpronounceable first sound) became *alpha*, for the vowel sound of A.

Hĕ (with a first sound that the Greek tongue had trouble with) became *ĕ*. To stretch the name out, for it seemed too short, it was referred to as *ĕ-psilon*, which means "merely e."

Khēth (with a bothersome first sound) became *ēta*, with about the sound of our long E.

'ayin (with its impossible initial sound) became Greek *ō-ĕ*; later to be called *ō-micron*, meaning "little ō."

That left two. Both of these ended up as vowels, though they had been consonants with the Phoenicians. To us those same letters are sometimes vowels in the Greek manner, sometimes consonants as with the Phoenicians—because of Roman practice.

Yodh became Greek *ī-ota*. The Phoenicians started the word with the tongue curled up against the top of the mouth; the Greeks kept the mouth open. And we can do either one—for the Y as a consonant or the I as a vowel.

Waw became *ū* or *ū-psilon* ("merely ū"). The Phoenicians started the word with the lips puckered and the mouth almost closed, as in our W sound. The Greeks kept their puckered lips open, giving the sound about that of our U in "use."

(The western Greeks could pronounce the W sound as well as the Ū sound. For the first they put in a special letter symbol that was to develop into our F; it was called *di-gamma,* for it was made from two gammas meshed together.)

And that was the way the Greek list of letters with its six vowels came into being—such an unstudied thing, apparently, with the vowels there almost by accident. And yet, strangely enough, how complete. So few Greek sounds had been missed!

Kadmus probably never told his Greek friends that *'aleph* meant "ox," that *beth* was for "house," that *gamal* was "camel." And had he done so, they would have paid no attention. To them "ox" was *bous,* not *'aleph* or *alpha.* A house was *oikia,* not *beth* or *beta.* And they knew nothing about camels, never having seen any. Not realizing that the first letter was a simple picture of an ox head, the Greeks were soon to turn the head with the nose up and to lop off the ears, in making A. They thought it looked better that way. The house picture of the second letter was closed at the bottom to make it into a sort of two-story apartment; in that way it looked less like their *rho* and resembled quite closely our B. The sea-waves of the Phoenician *mem* were changed from curves to rigid saw-teeth. The tooth picture was turned on edge. And there were other minor changes. But the original

Phoenician

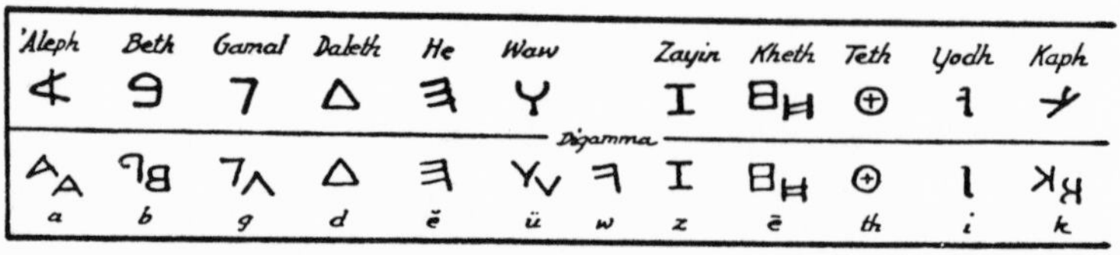

'Aleph	Beth	Gamal	Daleth	He	Waw		Zayin	Kheth	Teth	Yodh	Kaph
⤢	⅁	7	△	⅌	Y		I	⊟н	⊕	⅂	⤲
ᴧA	⅃ʙ	�7ᴧ	△	⅌	Yᴗ	ꓯ	I	⊟н	⊙	⅂	ᴋᴴ
a	b	g	d	ē	ü	w	z	ē	th	i	k

Digamma

forms of the pictures of the objects of Phoenicia had set their stamp upon the symbols of the Greeks, as anyone may see when the letter forms are placed side by side.

Alpha to Omega

In the days of Kadmus the Greeks wrote from right to left, as the Phoenicians did. Later they varied the plan by writing one line to the left, the next to the right, then one again to the left—as a person would plow a field. Finally, around the year 500 B.C., they settled upon the left-to-right manner as being the best. And our letters face the way they do, and our writing follows the direction we consider correct, because the Greeks of twenty-five centuries ago decided the matter for us.

I used to think that all the Greeks of Hellas spoke in exactly the same way. I was wrong. Those who had come by land into Hellas had never pronounced their words exactly as did those who came south by sea. Now Kadmus had worked with the western Greeks, and the early alphabet of Greek letters fitted their needs quite well. It did not do so well with the eastern Greek people. Around 500 B.C. some changes were made by the eastern group, in which a few new letters were added, a few old ones were dropped, and the sounds

and early Greek letters.

Lamed	Mem	Nun	Samekh	'Ayin	Pe	Tsade	Qoph	Rosh	Shin	Taw
ㄴ	ㄩ	ㄣ	丰	O	ㄱ	ㄏ	ㅇ	ㄱ	W	+
			Xi			*San*			*Sigma*	
ㄴ	ㄲ	ㄲ	丰	Oʘ	ㄲ	ㄇ	ㅇ	ㄱ	⟨	T
l	*m*	*n*	*x*	*o*	*p*	*s*	*k,q*	*r*	*s*	*t*

represented by a few were changed. The changed list is known today as the classical Greek alphabet and is the one in official use in modern Greece. In it the Ō sound was given two symbol forms and names to match: ō-*micron*, "little ō"; ō-*mega*, "big ō." In it, but not in the western list, the symbol H was for a vowel. In it the *pi* had the shape of a footstool; in it the *xi* did not look like our X, but *chi*, a new letter, did.

Examples of Greek writing. At the very top the direction of writing is from right to left in Phoenician style. Now watch the direction that the E's face. In example 3 the top line runs to the right, the next line to the left, the next to the right—just as if one were plowing a field. In the lowest example the direction is that of all later Greek writing, from left to right.

From it the *digamma* and *koppa* were omitted, for they were not needed; but *phi* and *psi* had been added to get in some east-Greek sounds.

In all parts of the Greek world a knowledge of the art of writing turned out to be a matter of importance to everyone. The people were readily thrilled by the tales of heroes. Long poems about the Trojan War and the wanderings of Ulysses, which in earlier times had been memorized and so passed from one generation to the next, were written down. Schools were set up in which reading and writing were taught, with much time spent in the memorizing and delivery of the great warrior poems. The Greeks, then, used their writing to preserve a national literature. In doing so they kept the letter forms intact.

From early Greek to classical Greek

A	B	Γ	Δ	Ε	Ι	Θ	⊙	I	K	Λ	M
A	B	Γ	Δ	E	Z	H	θ	I	K	Λ	M
Alpha	Beta	Gamma	Delta	Epsilon	Zeta	Eta	Theta	Iota	Kappa	Lambda	Mu

N	∓	O	Γ	Ϙ	P	⟨	T	Y	Φ	X	Ψ	⊙
				(koppa)								
N	Ξ	O	Π		P	Σ	T	Y	Φ	X	Ψ	Ω
Nu	Xi	Omicron	Pi		Rho	Sigma	Tau	Upsilon	Phi	Chi	Psi	Omega

CHAPTER 5

The Rise of Rome

Building an Alphabet

This is the story of ancient Rome and the little country of the Latins. In a sense it is also the story of their prosperous, slave-owning neighbors to the north, the Etruscans, who in early Roman days had entered northern Italy, driving the older inhabitants back to the hills or enslaving them. The people of the Latin tribe, hemmed in by mountains and the sea, had no place to go. They had to fight back or be annihilated. The Tiber River, running westward toward the sea, became their northern boundary. Rome, built on some low hills beside the river, guarded well the bridge to the Etruscan country and so was the sole point of contact between the Latins and the outer world.

For three centuries little Rome remained an unimpressive army outpost. Then, as it steadily gained in power, its soldiers were to wipe out, one by one, the Etruscan cities. A century and a half later would find Roman soldiers in northern Africa and Greece. Still later the Roman legions would be marching along the wide-spreading highways of the Roman world.

The Romans had many fine qualities. Their habits of life

Etruscan sportsman

gave them healthy bodies. Certainly every true Roman was
thoroughly disgusted with the prosperous Etruscans across
the Tiber who indulged in rich foods and then built swimming pools and gymnasiums to work off the flabby fat. In
fact any Roman would have been dismissed from the army if
he had behaved like an Etruscan businessman and ridden
downtown to his office instead of walking briskly as befitted
a true man. But the Etruscans had their good points also.
It was from them that the Romans got the ideas of paved
streets, sewers, and aqueducts. From them the Romans got
the thought of the circus and the chariot race, the purple
border of the toga, the observance of conquests with celebra-
tions. Their laws formed the basis of Roman law; their military system was a model for the Romans.

It was from the Etruscans that the Romans got their writing plan. These people had brought their alphabet with them
when they first came to Italy, and from it the Roman alphabet

was developed. The Etruscan arrangement was a very early Greek one that had all twenty-two of the Phoenician letters in their original order, with four Greek letters as extras. The writing was in Phoenician style, from right to left. To fit this particular alphabet, with its mixture of Phoenician and early Greek letters, to the Latin language of the Romans needed the guiding hand of some Kadmus.

The alphabet, as produced by the Romans, had one very peculiar feature. There were three letters for the single sound of K. Part of the blame for this situation can be ascribed to the Etruscans. They could not pronounce clearly the first sound in the Phoenician *gamal* (or the Greek *gamma*). They made it sound about like the K of *kaph*. For example, they would have said "Gay" and "Kay" in the same way. When we pronounce the two names we add a sort of grunt to the first sound in "Gay," and leave it out in "Kay." The Etruscans did not put the grunt in. That gave them two letters with the soft-K sound. And the Romans, not knowing what else to do, kept them both. You will recall that the Phoenicians gave an emphatic K sound to their *qoph*, a sound that was about like the K in our "Look!" The Romans could not detect much difference between this K and the soft K. But, not sensing what else to do, they kept it too.

The sensible thing for the Romans to have done was to keep the soft K of *kaph*, dropping the others. But they left

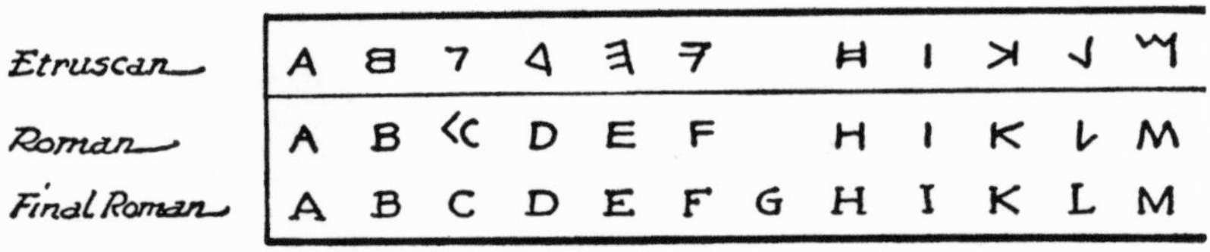
Etruscan
Roman
Final Roman
A B C D E F G H I K L M

in all three. The C, as the symbol for the old *gamal*, was called *kē*; the K, as the symbol for the old *kaph*, was named *kay*; the Q, as the symbol for the old *qoph*, was *kū*. They used the first as the K sound in most words, reserved the second for a few special words, kept the third for all words in which a U followed the K sound. (And the worst part, from our standpoint, is that we have never extricated ourselves from this confusion. We write "cat, "king," and "queen," using three letters with the sound of one!)

Now for the C-G story.

By the year 300 B.C. the Etruscan influence on the Latin alphabet was a thing of the past. The Romans were coming in contact with a Greek world, where the writing was done from left to right. The Greeks could distinguish between "gay" and "kay," and the Romans found that they could do so too. So in 312 B.C. the Latin alphabet was enlarged to take in the *gay*, as the new letter was to be called. For its symbol a line was drawn across that used for C (kē) to make the G. It went into the alphabet, not in the third position where the Phoenician *gamal* had been, but into the seventh place where, *zayin* had been located. (The Romans had dropped the *zayin*. They thought it was not needed. Later this letter with the Z sound was put back in; it had to go to the very end of the list, for its old place had been given to the G.)

(1)

CORNELIOL·F·SCIPIO
IDILES·COSOL·CESOR

(2)

IMP·CAESARI·DIV
TRAIANO·AVG·G

(3)

These examples might be given the title, "Seven centuries of Latin (Roman) writing." The top one, on a gold brooch of about 600 B.C., was probably written by an Etruscan jeweler, but the words are in Latin. The second is a funerary inscription of F. Cornelius Scipio, 259 B.C. Neither the spelling nor all of the letter shapes have reached their final forms. The third is a portion of the memorial to Emperor Trajan.

It is hard to explain how the Romans got into the P-R difficulty, in which the symbol for one letter was transferred to another letter. But in some little-understood way the Romans got to using the P symbol, which belonged to the Phoenician *rosh*, not only for the *rosh* but also for the Phoenician *pe*. Then, when they realized the confusion, a line was added to the P when the *rosh* was intended, giving the new letter form of R. Of course it was the wrong one that was changed; the *rosh* should have kept the P form. And that is why the Greek alphabet and modern-language alpha-

Black wax diptych

bets based upon the Greek have a different sound for their P symbol from that used in Western Europe and the Americas.

And now for the final bit of confusion in alphabet-building.

Up to Roman times a letter stood for one sound, not for two different sounds. The Romans broke that rule twice. In one case the confusion was not great and the matter was straightened up about fifteen centuries later by inserting an extra letter to handle one of the two sounds. The Romans assigned both the Phoenician consonant sound of the *yodh* and the Greek vowel sound of *i-ota* to the letter I.

The Romans were badly confused in the other case. This related to the sixth letter of the Phoenician list, for which the symbol was a simple picture of a metal hook (Ψ), and the letter carried the sound of our W. The Greeks had used the symbol for the vowel sound of *ū-psilon*, which almost matched our U sound in "use." To make the Romans' story short, they used the symbol V, made from the old metal-hook picture, for both *ŭ* and *vee*, though these sounds were totally unlike. They kept Y, also made from the metal-hook picture, for the Greek *ū-psilon*. And where the Phoenician W letter had been in the alphabet list they put the *digamma* symbol, F, and called it *ef*. (The western Greeks had used the *digamma* for the W sound.)

A *Diploma* for *Caesar*

In the days of her military glory the people of Rome were no longer the illiterate persons they had been a few centuries before. In fact, the Age of Augustus was a great period in Roman literature, when the writers gained a fame for Rome that approached that of Athens in the days of her glory. The usual writing material of the time was papyrus from Egypt. Wound upon sticks, each important roll (or *volumen*, to use the Roman word) needed a case (or *capsa*) to protect the writing. But for a homely recording of daily doings a special form of tablet was used that reminds us of the schoolroom slates of an earlier America. This tablet was made of a flat piece of wood with a raised margin. In the center a layer of black wax would be spread. Writing was done by making marks in the wax down to the white wood below, with a wood or ivory stylus. If an error was made in the writing the matter was easily handled. The white lines of the writing could be smoothed out with the round rear end of the stylus. To clear the tablet for another message the wax would be softened over a candle flame. The white marks would disappear.

To protect the writing upon the black wax surface, two tablets might be attached at the edges so they could fold face to face. This was called a *diptych*; it had *two* parts, and di meant "two." But neither a sheet of papyrus nor a double wax tablet was very useful for writing that needed to be preserved. So in very special cases and for very important things the wood of the tablet was replaced by white ivory, and the writing would be engraved down into the ivory itself, the letters being darkened for easy reading. The marks could not then be changed or erased. It was the custom of the Roman Senate to issue such an engraved-ivory diptych to an important general or noted official in granting him special rights or powers. And they would make quite a ceremony of the matter, calling the thing issued a *diploma*.

Centuries later the universities of Europe were to revive the idea of the diploma and the ceremony of diploma-giving. The writing was in Latin, and certain rights and privileges were granted—largely the privilege of writing A.B. after the name and paying alumni dues. Such a diploma was not made in *two* parts (and so might better have been called a *ploma*). It contained no ivory, the writing being on a sheepskin parchment. Today even the Latin may be gone from the diploma. The formal wording that once copied the phrases of the Roman Senate may also be gone. And paper may be used for the parchment. How times have changed! But the style of lettering has changed even more than the materials upon which the writing is made. Only the capital letters of the diploma look like the formal letters cut on the memorial arches of long-ago Rome.

CHAPTER 6

Trailing the Roman Letters

Small Letters from Big

The Romans used only the letter forms that we call *capitals*. Who, then, developed the small-letter forms? And why? The answers are to be found in the story of *parchment*, a new writing material that came into use late in Roman Empire days. It was expensive stuff, so used only for highly important work. It was quite heavy, though flexible—almost cumbersome, rather than light like papyrus. Its use demanded a new kind of bookmaking. But as it never became fragile with age, it might be expected to last indefinitely if kept in any well-ventilated place free from mice, tiny beetles, and bookworms.

Parchment was made from the hides of sheep. After the wool was off, the skin was split into sheets. (That was the tricky part.) Then the sheets were soaked for several days in slaked lime to take out the oil and decayable parts and leave just the tough fibers. When the unused lime had been removed by a thorough washing, each sheet was stretched on a frame to dry. The parchment-making was completed by scraping each sheet to an even thickness, dusting with chalk, then rubbing smooth with pumice stone. Vellum, a softer and even more expensive writing material, was made from antelope hides. Both parchment and vellum took ink marks well; the pigment soaked into the surface slightly but did not spread sideways. This gave the written strokes great permanency. Mistakes could be made right only by scraping away the surface with a sharp knife, then repolishing the roughened place before the corrections were inserted.

The thousand years that followed this invention have been called the Era of Parchment-and-the-Pen. In this era the writing styles of Western Europe shifted away from the formal and dignified capitals to the simpler, smaller, and more rounded letter forms made so readily with pen strokes on parchment. In a political way this era was a tempestuous one. It had begun with Constantine and his establishment of Christianity as the official religion of Rome, followed by a burst of missionary zeal that carried the religion to every Roman province. Then, later, the western Roman Empire disintegrated as pagan tribes swept across the Rhine and Danube. The old civilization seemed to disappear along with the blazing homes, the looted cities, and the destroyed churches. Yet in a mere century or so some of the pagan chieftains were converted to Christianity. Little by little churches and monasteries were built again. And the art of reading and writing, kept alive in the church and monastery schools, again flourished.

One may well wonder how it was accomplished, but every religious organization of the time, no matter how small, possessed a parchment copy of some fragment of the Bible or some religious epistle. Such a copy had to be prepared from an earlier copy lent for a short time for the purpose. If the

copy lent was a portion of the Bible, it itself had been made
from some still earlier copy, and so on almost endlessly. It
probably was as difficult then as it is today to copy a long
passage by hand and have it come out *exactly* correct. Certainly the chainlike copyings of Bible passages in many cases
introduced errors at some point down the line. A line omitted
would stay omitted. Some added comment might be considered a part of the original by the next copyist, in turn to
be copied by later copyists.

In the printed copy of the Bible that I have before me
there are 985 pages of text. Each page has two columns,
each column somewhat over 400 words. The total is about
800,000 words, perhaps *four million letters*. What a TRE-
MENDOUS task it must have been to make a handwritten copy
of the entire Bible, or even of some major portion of it. How
many sheep would be needed for the parchment, how many
workers besides the book scribes to get the job done! Only
an energetic and very vigorous religious organization with
great reserve supplies might be expected even to make the
try. And should such a monumental task be undertaken,
how much forethought would have to be given in advance
to the appearance of the finished page! Novel features of
letter forms might be introduced if those in charge were
gifted artists.

At three separate places in Western Europe in the two
centuries from A.D. 630 to 830 there were religious groups
that began, and completed, the writing out of the whole Bible
or of some major portion of it. Each book so prepared was
a masterpiece of handwritten art; each offered a novel, beautifully designed alphabet of letter forms. And, fortunately,

each as a bound volume has come down to us intact, zealously
preserved through the intervening centuries. The three—
virtually priceless—are the Book of Kells, the Lindisfarne
Gospels, and the Alcuin Bible. The first was created a thousand years ago by the strong religious organization on the
island of Iona, off the coast of Scotland in the Irish Sea. It
is now in the museum of the University of Dublin. The second, produced about a century later near York in northern
England, was hidden away when the Danes, swooping in
from the sea, destroyed Lindisfarne Chapel. It is now in the
British Museum. The third, produced somewhat later at
Lyons in southern France, contained the entire Bible. More
widely copied than the other two, this third book had an influence on later letter forms that was very great.

To show the artistic nature of the letters introduced by
these three great books, I give each ample space. As a sort of
introduction I show you first the parchment writing of pre-
Iona days. (I think you should be told right away that the

ΑBCδEFGhIRLm
NOpqRSTUΛYZ

*There was something very attractive about the rounded uncial
forms. Notice the change in appearance of the A; it reminds me
of the old Phoenician ox-head picture. Other uncial features were
the strongly rounded D, M, and V; the simplified H; the eight
letters having strokes that ended beyond the line of writing.*

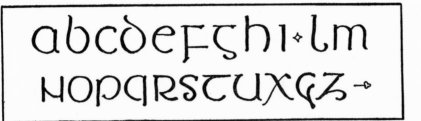

The lettering in the Book of Kells was even more attractive than that of the uncial scribe. I like the handling of the a, b, e, l, m, t, and y. An oddity of this alphabet was the absence of k. In their copying of the Latin Bible this letter did not occur.

> Et non potuerunt
> uerbum eius
> repraeheiroere—

In the Lindisfarne Gospels the style of writing follows quite closely that of the Book of Kells. In the example shown the scribes seem to have been experimenting with the form of the R.

quidiligitdmdiligat et fratrem suum·
Omnisquicreditqnmiiis·e·xps·exdonatus·e·etomnis
quidil
Inhocs

abcdefghiklmnopqrstuxyz

The Alcuin minuscules had some peculiarities besides their much smaller size. Note the elongated s, the stiffened d, the g with the small top and the long twisting tail, and the return to the uncial a. The quotation shows the Alcuin way of ending sentences and beginning new sections. Lines over letters indicate abbreviations.

letters of the Alcuin Bible were to give us our *printed small letters*. Perhaps in the Lindisfarne letter forms you may glimpse some features of our *penmanship letters*.)

Some comments about Alcuin himself, as well as about his Bible, are in order. Counted as the greatest Bible scholar in Western Europe, he was in York, England, when an urgent message reached him from Charlemagne, ruler of what is now France. The fiery monarch had been informed that many of the churches and monasteries of his country had copies of parts of the Bible that contained errors. (He himself could not read or write, but signed his name with an X, which meant he was a Christian.) He had been given to understand that some of the errors were grievous matters. Something ought to

Charlemagne

be done about it. He wanted Alcuin to take full charge, to make needed revisions. He offered him ample funds and full authority. Alcuin accepted, set up a special training school for scribes at Lyons, and put into use the minuscule letter forms designed especially for the new project. His school at

Lyons carried all writing across a wide column, using a dot to end each sentence. (This idea was new in Western Europe.) Each new sentence was begun with a large-sized letter, each section with a still larger one set in the margin. These large-size letters were not capitals but merely oversize minuscules.

For the titles of the books of the Bible, Alcuin used letter forms from the old triumphal arches. But that was his sole use of the dignified capital letters. Later book scribes were to give these letters some additional work to do. They were to be used for new sentences and new sections. They were to be used for personal names. And the English scribes were even to use a capital for that unabashed personal pronoun I. (But a little i standing all by itself wouldn't look right!)

Handmade Books

After Alcuin's time the copying of religious writings became a matter of big business for some of the larger monasteries. A special place was set aside for it, the *scriptorium*. Each copyist was a *scriba*, the completed book a *liber manu scriptus* ("book by-hand written"). We have the two expressions as "scribe" and "manuscript."

The workshop of the scribes was likely to be the space above the hall of the chapter house. I am ready to concede that the conditions would be pleasant enough in summer with the windows open, and satisfactory in late spring and early fall. But not in winter! Lest some priceless manuscript be damaged by a spark or ruined by an overturned candle, no fireplace was put in the room, and no candles could be used near a work table. A lighted charcoal brazier for warming the hands was permitted, but far away from the copying.

The scriptorium might have carried quite appropriately the sign QUIET, MEN AT WORK. Only gestures were allowed. The person in charge passed out the sheets of parchment and the supply of pens, ink, knives, awls, and rulers. The awls were to hold the sheets in place, the knives for scraping out mistakes in the writing. The parchment was given out in sections, each sheet folded and arranged in the position it would take in the finished work. The scribe would begin on the sheet by ruling off margins. Then he would put in the guide lines for the writing, using a blunt stylus that made a slight furrow in the sheet. The writing was done in a black ink. This was a monastery product, made from a concoction

Monk copying a manuscript

Monastery reading room

of barks and various other things, boiled for hours before straining. After four sheets had been finished, each folded to give two pages, the writing was proofread to catch possible errors. Then the sheets were passed on to the *rubricator*, a specialist. You might have preferred his job to that of the scribe. He put in titles and headlines, added decorative borders in red, gold, or blue, and inserted needed notes. (The gold was real metal!) After that the sheets were ready for binding. Early monastery books had been fastened with leather strips passed through special holes in the parchment sheets and knotted at the back. Later, board covers were put on for outside protection and to keep the sheets from tearing. Pieces of well-tanned leather covered both the boards and the leather ends. Finally, metal clasps were added to the covers to keep the parts firmly in position when the book was not in use. This was of importance, for the books were bulky and heavy.

It will be realized that the making of a book demanded many workers besides those of the scriptorium. The sheets of parchment had to be prepared from the skins of great flocks of sheep; the black ink made; colored pigments secured for

The scriptorium did not make a good working place in winter. It could be both dark and cold; one was hard on the eyes, the other hard on the disposition.

the rubricator; calfskin tanned for the covers; metal clasps fashioned for the finished book. To keep such a book from being carelessly left where it might be damaged by mold or destroyed by mice, each monastery had a reading room with the books *fastened to the shelves by light chains.*

By Wen and Thorn

We have been reporting on Latin writing for Latin Bibles. In telling the story of English writing with English words, we shall begin with Alfred the Great, who was King of the West Saxons in the late ninth century, about a century later than the days of Charlemagne. He seems to have been quite proud of his people, for he wrote a history of England, not in Latin, as he might have done, but in the language of England. True, he used Latin letters in the writing. But he also included two *pagan* ones. He had not been responsible for letting the odd letters get in, but he made no effort to oust them. *They were needed and, being needed, stayed.*

The story of how they got into the English alphabet goes back a century and a half before Alfred was born. In that distant time, about the year 700, a traveling minstrel went from place to place across central England, singing, to the strumming of his lute, the hero tales of the northland. A favorite with his listeners was the epic poem of the doings of Beowulf-the-Mighty, who killed a dragon with his bare hands and the mother of the dragon with his trusty sword. A monk, who had learned Latin in a church school and the pagan way of writing from an old Druid priest, tried to get down on parchment the minstrel's song in the words of the singer.

peoɲca þonne ʒpendel hine ɲoɲ þan ic
hine ſpeoɲðe ſpebban nelle alðɲe benea
can þeah ic eal mœʒe nāꝽ he þaɲa ʒoða

This is English as written in 1000, in a copy of the old poem
Beowulf. *The first letter of the first word is the runic* wen, *the*
first letter of the second word is the runic thorn. *You may scarcely*
believe it, but the last two words of the quotation are not papa
soda, *but* thara goda!

There were two important letter sounds in the north-country
speech not found in the Latin. They were, however, on the
pagan list. So the monk put the extra letters in for the sounds
needed. It was a strange thing to do, perhaps, but it was useful. And others who wrote in the language of old England
followed the monk's plan and kept the two pagan letters
among the others.

The inserted letters had the Saxon names of *wen* and *thorn*.
Each represented the sound that formed the first part of the
name. The first of the letters was for the W sound so common in English words but unused in Latin. The second
needs some comment and some discussion of what the tongue
can do. In our words "thorn," "think," "thick," and so on,
the first sound is made with the tongue out beyond the edge
of the teeth. This is not the way the Greeks handled their
theta; for it the tongue was against the front of the mouth,
just above the back side of the teeth. And it is not the way
the Romans handled their TH sound, in which the tongue
tip was held tightly to the roof of the mouth to be pulled

away sharply as the sound was made. Perhaps you did not realize that the tongue could do so many tricks. There is still another. The first sound of our words "the," "those," and "them" is really not that of *thorn*, in spite of our present-day spelling. For it the tongue is pressed firmly against the back side of the teeth, then a D sound is made through the nose as the tongue is pulled back. This makes the sound DH, not TH. Alfred the Saxon recognized this when he used for it a minuscule D with a line across the vertical stroke—a *barred D*, as the old form is now called.

Both the *barred D* and the *thorn* are now gone. The first was absorbed into the second by the English writers. Then the English *thorn*, the Greek *theta*, and the Latin TH were merged by scribe and printer, in spite of the wide differences in pronunciation. Yet, in a sense, the *thorn* has never fully disappeared. Just before the invention of printing the old pagan letter form had become Y-shaped; the real Y carried a dot over it to avoid confusion. The earliest English printers kept both the Y-shaped *thorn* and the dotted Y. Next the dot disappeared and the Y did duty for both. You will find the old *thorn* operating in disguise when the printer runs off a card with "Ye old-fashioned greetings" printed on it. And if you are properly old-fashioned (and recognize the *thorn*) you will read the message in the old-fashioned way as "*The* old-fashioned greetings."

The *wen* did not last as a part of the English alphabet as long as the *thorn*. It was changed to a "double U" by the Norman-French clerks. And from them the changed letter passed into current English use. You see, the clerks did not pronounce the W sound as the Saxons had done. They did

> ꝥ þe bigynnyng was þe word ꞇ þe word was
> at god · ꞇ god was þe word / þis was in þe bigȳ
> nyng at god / alle þingis weren maad bi hym:

This is English as written in 1400, in Wycliffe's Bible. By this time the wen had been dropped in favor of W, but the thorn remained. The passage given is the starting sentence of the Gospel of John: "In the bigynnyng was the word and the word was . . ." The thorn, in the combination thorn-e, appears three times in this first line; the w as W, four times. (The y carries a dot over it, but the i does not.)

not pucker the lips closely but kept the mouth a little open. So their sound came out as ōō-ŭ. In writing this down they used U for the ōō part, then added another U for the ŭ. This gave them UU or W. And that is the way the letter has remained.

We might say something about the Runic alphabet, from which the *wen* and *thorn* were taken. There is uncertainty as to when this alphabet was invented and where. But it may be almost as old as the Latin alphabet itself, for there are some old Etruscan letter forms in it and some Greek forms as they might have been written by Greek traders. But the peculiar letter sounds of the north-country people are in there too, shown by forms of distinctive shape. Each letter of the list was given the name of some common thing that began with the sound. The U-sound letter was called *ur-ox* after a scraggy wild ox. The *thorn* was then, as now, the sharp point of a rosebush or haw tree (hawthorn tree). For easy

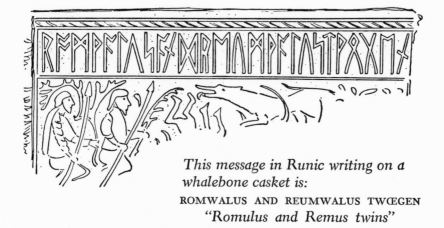

This message in Runic writing on a whalebone casket is:

ROMWALUS AND REUMWALUS TWŒGEN
"Romulus and Remus twins"

The wen *for* W, *which appears three times, looks much like our* P. *The* thorn *does not appear in this passage. The design on the casket side refers to a legend of the founding of Rome, in which a wolf acts as foster-mother to the orphaned twins. Only the legs of the boys are to be seen as they leap, like frightened animals, out of sight.*

memorizing the letters were arranged in a list that formed a rhyming jingle. You may remember Edgar Allan Poe's reference to it in "The Bells":

Keeping time, time, time
In a sort of Runic rhyme . . .

Runic writing disappeared in England and the north countries after the coming of Christianity, though the *barred D* and the *thorn* are still in the printers' fonts in Iceland. The Runic-written words on the whalebone casket shown above go back a thousand years or more.

Black-Letter Days

The historical scene for manuscript-writing now shifts
from France and England to Germany, Holland, and the
Flemish countries. The time is about the year 1240. The
women of Lübeck have already begun to "high-hat" one another, for each is allowed to wear a hat whose height is a
measure of the wealth of her merchant-husband. It was a
time of great cathedral-building also, when the commercial
cities of Hamburg, Cologne, Bruges, and the rest were high-
hatting one another as to the loftiness of the spires they raised
toward the skies.

It was a time, too, when many people wanted their writings
put down on parchment. But the things to be put in writing
were held back by the parchment supply. Parchment came

from sheepskins. And there just *were
not enough sheep*. Then a book scribe
did some experimenting. Using a broad-
nibbed pen that made heavy strokes
when drawn downward and thin lines
sidewise, he found that he could pack
the minuscule letters much closer, and
set the writing lines nearer together
without loss of legibility. Soon every
book scribe was making these "black-
letter" forms and conserving parchment. After a century or so of the early,
simple black-letter writing, a change
gradually took place in letter forms.

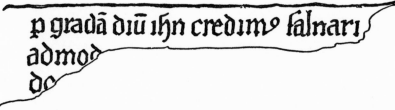

How strongly these minuscule black-letter forms show up on the manuscript page! With a broad-nibbed pen that made broad downward strokes and thin horizontal lines, the words could be packed closely and still be legible.

Extra lines were added to the letters, and initial letters were loaded with intricate scrolls. To make the matter worse, nearly all long words were being abbreviated and some of the short ones as well. Only to the expert were writing and reading now really easy.

In time the great cathedral-building days came to an end. And this was about the time when schools were spreading beyond monastery walls, when there was a new interest in poetry and drama and a deep change in religious thought. In Italy this time brought also a new interest in the old Greek

$$\mathfrak{ABCDEFGHIKLMN}$$
$$\mathfrak{OPQRSTUXYZ}.$$
$$\mathfrak{abcdefghiklmnopqrstu\,xyz}.$$

This is highly ornate "Old English." Eventually the early black-letter forms lost their simplicity. The capitals in particular became crowded with an elaboration of extra lines, which made writing slow and reading difficult.

and Roman authors and a hunting through old records of history. (We can scarcely realize how little the people of the year 1400 knew about the story of ancient Rome. Where the *Campus Martius* had been was but a cow pasture, for the dirt of the centuries had covered the old structures. Sometimes a farmer, digging a well, would find a statue or a stone-paved corridor or a marble faun. And people would wonder.)

The interest in old writings included an interest in the earlier book-writing styles and led to a rediscovery of the beauty of the Alcuin minuscules. Then the book scribes of Italy, catching the new enthusiasm for old things, laid aside the broad-nibbed pens to copy again the letter forms of six centuries before. We may smile now at the names given by the enthusiasts of the new order to the work done in the cathedral-building time. In their phraseology both the cathe-

The Italian scribes in the fourteen-hundreds went back to the minuscule letters of Alcuin, giving them the name of roman letters. Only the t and i did not revert to the centuries-old patterns; the first now had a short upward projection to keep it from resembling a c; the second carried a small stroke above it to avoid confusion of the letter with a stroke of the u or n.

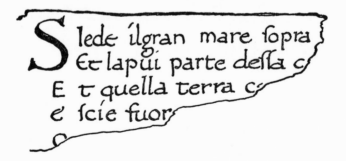

drals and the writing of the period were "uncouth," "barbaric," or "Gothic," though the era had really been one of bold engineering, sound workmanship, and excellent, though somber, design. The new order was "humanistic" or "Roman." But the letter forms were no more Roman than the others had been Gothic, though both names have lasted on.

CHAPTER 7

Going to Press

Paper from China

In the year 1200 even a rich monastery would have had a library of less than 150 books, many of these more pamphlets than books. And the situation had scarcely changed two centuries later. It was not so much that people did not want to read and write, not so much that people had no important thoughts to write down. *Parchment was just too hard to get.* As writing materials, many things beside parchment and the pen had, of course, been tried. But something better was needed; some greater human inventiveness was wanted.

One of nature's creative specialists has been the paper wasp. Chewing up some wood fibers, mixing in a supply of water-repellent, insect-made mucilage to hold the fibers together, then spreading the product out in sheets, the female wasp quickly rears the tough but thin walls of her nursery. It seems easy as I tell about it. And the hornet, working the same tricks, makes for her baby hornets a veritable apartment house. Perhaps no human inventor found in the procedures of these insects a clue to his own need for paper. But the Egyptians had developed their papyrus sheets along the same

lines as the insects, when they covered them with a cooked
mass of vegetable gum. Then, a thousand years later, the
Chinese worked a similar plan with linen fibers and an excellent grade of vegetable gum and turned out a product better than papyrus. And Europe, which had no supply of
papyrus plants but could raise flax for linen, and wanted
something better than the weak and brittle product from
Egypt, was to find in *paper from China* the answer to many
problems.

You may have seen Chinese paper—unusually soft, yet
exceedingly tough, pure white, of an even texture. It certainly does not look at all like a linen handkerchief or a
scarf, for the linen fibers are matted, not woven. It will not
be a matter of surprise, then, that those who wanted to know
—and wanted badly—how the Chinese made their paper
never dreamed that the stuff was made from the linen fibers
of flax. After developing a market for their paper in the Far
East, the Chinese sent loads of it to the West over the long
caravan route that crossed the Asian continent. Great trading
centers such as Constantinople, just off the Black Sea, and
Baghdad, on the Tigris, bought the Chinese product at really
premium prices.

At this particular time in history Baghdad was the leading
city of a Moslem world that stretched from Turkestan in the
east on through Egypt and northern Africa to the Atlantic
Ocean in the west. And Baghdad wanted very much to know
the Chinese paper-making secret. Help came in an unex-
pected way. To avoid transportation costs the Chinese, in
time, transferred the paper-making headquarters to Chinese
Turkestan. This was a political mistake. The new location was

too close to Moslem borders. By spying, extortion, and bribery the men of Baghdad finally discovered the Chinese secrets, or at least enough of them to get started on their own manufacture. Their greatest surprise was in finding that flax was the basic raw material. Now it should be noted that the Moslems were world-famous for the production of linens from flax. The inland city of Damascus, just east of the Lebanons, was a great producer, and so was Egypt. It was not difficult to shift some of the flax to paper-making, at first on an experimental scale. In a short time the Moslems directed their new efforts toward the production of paper for manuscript work; the softer Chinese paper had been excellent for many other uses. In fact, the new material proved so good for all writing purposes, and the possible supply was so unlimited, that the Moslem ruler of Egypt in the year 1200 is reported to have had a library of 100,000 rolls and pamphlets, all written on Moslem paper.

In 1276 the first paper mill to be started in any Christian country was opened at Fabriano in Italy. The product turned out was constant in quality and fully up to Moslem standards. Two steps in the Moslem-Chinese process had, to advantage, been modified. The first change came in using clean linen rags instead of flax fibers. (And after that the rag-pickers of Europe had a steady job.) The other was in substituting animal glues, in sizing, for the vegetable gums. Since we can seldom see in this country any paper made by hand processes, it may be well to describe the making of Fabriano paper, using an old picture.

In the vat in the foreground the clean linen rags have been soaked and then beaten gently until the woven fibers are well

Paper-making

loosened. This forms the *paper pulp*. The operator behind the
vat holds a *deckle*, a device with a wire screen at the bottom
to let water drain through. The deckle is dipped into the
pulp to pick up the fibers for a single sheet. A good operator
knows just how to move the deckle about in the vat to mat
and entangle the fibers thoroughly. Then out comes the
deckle, dripping water from the wet pulp. Upon being turned
upside down, the pulp sheet slips out of the deckle and drops
on a felt pad. You may hold your breath, thinking this step
is a mistake, for the pulp will surely mesh into the felt. But it
doesn't. The pad merely takes out much of the dampness.
Then on top goes another pad, then another sheet from the
pulp vat, then another pad, and so on. Eventually the pile
of sheets and pads will be shifted over to the second operator

and put in his press. Pressure will squeeze the surplus water from the sheets. Next comes the unscrambling part, and the sheets are now dry enough to be stacked one upon another. Under the press the stack goes; then the position of the stack is shifted, with another squeeze from the press. The sheets are now hung up, several in a group, to dry. Then down they come and are dipped in a gummy sizing, pressed, and hung again in groups for a final drying. And when the day's run is over the sheets are placed on the counter shelves at the side of the room, awaiting a shipping order. Every sheet carries a "deckle-edge," where the fibers thin away at the margins.

Go today into an art store and ask for fine drawing paper. If you get a full-sized sheet it will have the deckle-edge and the stamp of quality used in all handmade papers. But the steps in the making are today done by machinery. The watchful operator no longer needs to roll up his sleeves or wet his hands in the vat. Even the number of sheets is counted for

Chinese scribe

him as they pass through the machine. For a cheaper paper the great paper mills substitute wood pulp or cotton pulp for all or a part of the linen. The finished product is wound in great rolls. And that is the present-day ending for the story of paper-from-China.

Best-Sellers of 1500

Printing from movable type was perfected about 1440 by Johann Gutenberg; all the first printing was done in Germany with black-letter forms. But printing on a press had been done years before that. The lines of a song, the pictured figures of a religious tract, the numbers of a multiplication table—things like these had been chiseled in the surface of a block of wood or engraved on a sheet of metal. And the wood blocks or metal sheets had been used in a printing press to get many exact copies run off on paper. Printing as we know it came later.

One may wonder whether it was the *idea* of the use of movable type that made Gutenberg's invention so remarkable, or whether it was the way the idea was put to use. Let us see. Before a single page of printing could be run off, many things needed to be done. The letter forms to be used had to be decided upon and a punch constructed for each and every symbol that would be required for the printing. The projecting parts on these punches looked like the type on the type-bars of a present-day typewriter. The punches were then used in preparing matrices of the proper size and depth. By pouring melted type-metal into the matrices the type for the printing press was produced. Each matrix had to be used many times, for even one page set in type would require perhaps 125 E's, 75 A's, and so on. Finally some devices had to be designed and built for holding the type in position while the composition was being set and while it was in the press.

The printer of today buys such equipment. The early printer had to make everything for himself or pay someone to make it under his direction. It is true that much of the pioneering had already been done before Gutenberg's first press work. The printing press was modeled after a wine press. The letter forms for the printer's type were those of some manuscript writer. The letter punches were built along the lines of those used by coin-makers for the lettering on coins, and the matrices were like those of the coin-makers also. The casting metal and the casting procedure were those of the makers of medallions.

After one of the early printers had spent time and money in equipment, he would then be in a position to buy some

Johannes
Gutenberg

paper, to make some sticky printer's ink, and to set a composition in type. Having done all of these things, he would start his hand-operated press and be able to run off several hundred copies of the press job in a few days. And if he was a good judge of human nature he might find enough people to buy his printed product, and so meet expenses. Some of the printers actually made a profit. And the best-sellers in Gutenberg's part of Europe? *Arithmetics!* How to add, subtract, multiply, and divide with the new Arabic number symbols! Every business office in Germany seemed to want someone who could make business calculations. These arithmetics were *self-help* books.

In 1464 two German printers, Johann and Wendelin da Spira, took their press to Venice. The manuscript-writers of Italy had already developed the so-called roman letters for their book-writing. These printers tried out a type form modeled somewhat imperfectly after the forms of the manuscripts. In 1470 Nicolas Jenson, who had been a coin-maker to the king of France, went to Venice and set up as a printer. He was an expert in the making of punches for letter work, and the alphabet of minuscule and capital letters that he designed and constructed was highly superior. (I have heard printers argue that his type was the most perfect ever cut.)

The Venice of that day was a busy place; its shops were visited by buyers from every part of Europe. It was thus an excellent location for a printer as able and progressive as Jenson. It was an excellent location for that master printer Aldus Manutius, who was to follow Jenson as the leading printer of Venice. Aldus introduced such a type novelty as *italics* (based on the work of Italian penmen) , gave a more convenient and smaller size to his books, and set the price accordingly. He gained both reputation and wealth. And, oddly enough, his best-sellers were editions of old Greek and Latin authors!

From 1470, when Jenson first reached Venice, to the death of Aldus, half a century later, the work of the Venetian printers was the dominating influence in printing west of Germany. An effect of this was the establishment of roman type as standard for printing usage. As this type was based upon the best forms of the Italian book scribes of that time, and these, in turn, upon Alcuin's minuscule letters, the letter forms of Charlemagne's time had become again the dominant forms of all Christendom to the west of Germany. And that, of course, took in the British Isles.

ALDVS
MANVTIVS

Dots and Tails

That the minuscule letters of Alcuin were the models for those of Jenson and Aldus is entirely true. But that does not imply that there were no changes at all in the period from 800 to 1500. There were some. And there have been some in the four and a half centuries since the year 1500.

A cluster of changes was built around the letter I. The difficulty with this simplest of all letter strokes was that it was *too simple*. In the minuscule alphabet it was so little in size that it was often mistaken for *half* of a minuscule u or a minuscule n. And if there were two ii's in a row the confusion was complete. As a way out of this difficulty, some clever scribe put a small stroke over each minuscule i. Other scribes picked up the idea. The Italian scribes and the Venetian printers changed the stroke over the i to a dot. *And that is why we dot the i today.*

Going back to the idea of two minuscule i's in a row, another way of preventing them for being mistaken for a minuscule u or a minuscule n was to put a *tail* on the second i by a downward sweep of the pen. Thus *filii*, the Latin word for "sons," appeared as *filij*; its pronunciation had, of course, not changed, for the last letter was an i. The Dutch *miine*, for "mine," appeared as *mijne*. And such Roman numerals as 2, 3, 12, and 13, for example, were written ij, iij, xij, and xiij. (Your physician puts numbers like that on the prescriptions that he writes—along with his centuries-old Latin medical notations. Ask him if he uses accent marks over the i's, or whether he uses dots in Venetian style.)

The printer kept the tailed i in his font of letters, to be used occasionally. A tailed capital I with the form of J was there too. In the year 1600 the printers of Spain put the tailed forms of the letter to a new use. It will be remembered that the Romans had included two letter sounds under the letter symbol of I: a consonant sound that is like our Y, and the vowel sound of I. The Spanish printers broke that partnership by using the *regular I for the vowel*, the *tailed I for the consonant.* So the new letter J came into the Spanish alphabet, being placed just after I. In 1630 the English printers adopted the J (but not for the Y sound). But it was not until 1813 that the American dictionaries unscrambled "job," "judge," and "jury" from "ibex," "iron," and "indigo" and filed them under separate letters.

The Romans used such a spelling as IVLIVS *when they meant* JULIUS. *But that double use of the I and the double use of the V could have been confusing even to a Roman.*

U and Double U

Not found in the original Roman alphabet were two other letters that had found a place in our English alphabet earlier than the J. In Roman usage the V had played the strange double role of the vowel sound of our U and the consonant sound of our V. In parchment-writing days the Roman letter V, like other straight-lined letters, was given a new, curved look. It was now a U—though the name had not changed, or its dual-sound role. And when the Alcuin school at Lyons decided to keep the old formal Roman letters as capitals, the sharp V appeared in the titles; the rounded minuscule u was used in the rest of the writing. And that plan continued for hundreds of years.

Around the time when Colonial America was getting its

start the English printers had made the innovation of using
a large and small rounded form of U *just for the vowel sound*,
a large and small sharp-letter form of V *for the consonant
sound*. How simple! That, of course, made an additional
letter for the alphabet. The U was placed ahead of the V.

The W was the other letter to get into the English list.
We have briefly traced its story in recounting the fate of the
Runic *wen*. Actually the W was in the English list before
the U and V were separated. It was to be a "double U," but
its present-day shape is more double V than double U—a
matter that should have been looked after when U and V
became separated.

Menacrates and *Menas* famous Pyrates
Makes the Sea ferue them, which they eare and wound   *1623*
With keeles of euery kinde. Many hot inrodes

Menacrates and *Menas*, famous Pyrates
Makes the Sea ferve them, which they ear and wound   *1664*
With kneels of every kind. Many hot inrodes

*These passages from a play by Shakespeare seem exactly alike,
but the second and third lines differ slightly. In the printing of
1623 the minuscule u had to do double duty, in Roman style,
for u and v. In the 1664 printing separate letters are used for the
two, as in "serve," for "serue," and "every," for "euery."*

A *to Izzard*

We may bring the story of our letters nearer to a close by saying something about the names we have for these alphabet letters. As might be guessed, our English names were based on the Latin names for the letters. And the Latin names were, in general, those of the Etruscans. Using our English way of spelling the words, this is very close to the way the Latin names ran:

ah bay kee day ā ef gay hay ēē-yote kay
el em en oh pay koo er es tay ŏŏ-vay ix
ūpsilon zet

There are oddities in the names that we give to some of the letters. Our *aitch* is one of these. It started out as *hay*, in the Latin manner. After a while it was *haych*. Then *'aych*. And now *aitch*, with the H sound actually lost completely. There are two other oddities. Our U (for ŏŏ) is called *yoo*; that first sound of the name *does not belong*. Our Y is named *wi*; the first sound of this name *does not belong*. There are still other oddities, but in a different way. Latin *kee* for C has become English *see*. But we already had a letter *es*, for the S sound! Latin *gay* for G has become English *jee*. But we have a *jay* for that sound of J; we needed to keep the *gay*.

And now for something a little different. The last letter of the Latin alphabet carried the slightly shortened Greek name of *zet* (for *zeta*). In the present-day countries of Western Europe it normally appears under the name of *zet* or *zed*. In the France and England of half a thousand years ago it was sometimes referred to as *izzar* or *izzard*; just why, we do not

know. So the old English expression "from A to Izzard"
meant something complete. Today the people of Great Britain
call this last letter of our alphabet *zed*. We call it *zee*.

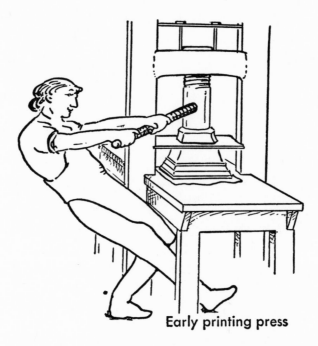

Early printing press

CHAPTER 8

The Printer
Carries On

Venice of the Mud Flats

In a previous section we mentioned briefly Aldus, the great printer of Venice, and the influence of the Venetians on printing styles. We must return to that topic, for the story both of Aldus and of Venice needs fuller handling.

For several important centuries the largest and most influential cities of Western Europe were the Italian cities

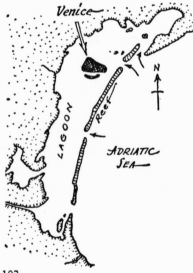

of Venice, Milan, Florence, and Genoa. And Venice was the most important of them all. The location of this city was a peculiar one. Near the northern curve of the Adriatic Sea and between the mouths of the Po and Piave Rivers is a long, narrow, almost continuous reef out about a mile from the main shore. Behind this reef is a rather shallow lagoon. And in the lagoon, on a cluster of mud-banks, is the city of Venice. Its houses were built on piles driven into the mud. Canals have taken the place of roads, gondolas of carriages.

In the year 1400 self-governed Venice was the most power-ful city of the western Mediterranean. As a trading center it was located at the heart of the commercial Europe of that day. To the north, over the Brenner Pass, ran the highway into Germany. Nearby, in Italy, were the inland cities of Milan and Florence, and much of their produce was handled by Venetian ships. At the eastern end of the Mediterranean, or near it, were the prosperous cities of a glamorous eastern world: Alexandria, Damascus, Constantinople, and Trebi-zond on the Black Sea. At these places there were cargoes of drugs, dyes, jewels, spices, and silks to be traded for fur from Russia, tin from England, fine cloth from Florence, and all the other products of the West handled by Venetian boats. (And there would sometimes be Venetian boats with women slaves for the Moslem harems.) In that year of 1400 Ven-ice was a place of seamen and merchants who dealt in the products of the Mediterranean trade. But it was also a place of skilled artisans who changed the raw products of one part of the world into beautiful and valuable manufactured prod-ucts for a world's trade. It is reported on good authority that 200,000 people were living in the city or on the shores near-by. The city had 45 warships, 300 large trading vessels, 3000 smaller ones, employing, in all, crews of 36,000 men. For the care of the ships there were 16,000 shipwrights. The area had also 3000 silk weavers and 16,000 wool weavers. The glass factories made the wonderful Venetian glass; the goldsmiths of Venice fashioned exquisite jewelry; her tailors set the clothing styles of the Western World. People from all the countries of Europe bought and sold in the lagoons of Venice.

Time has a way of upsetting the plans of cities and nations as well as of individuals. Just before the year 1500 Vasco da Gama, sailing under the flag of Portugal, reached India from Europe by going around Africa. After that ships from Portugal began to make regular trips to India and to bring the silk, spices, and drugs of the East directly to the ports of Western Europe. In the year 1504 there were no spices, dyes, and drugs from India to be transshipped to Venetian boats at Alexandria in Egypt, for all had been sold in India to the Portuguese. That year, for the first time, the ships of Venice and of Genoa sailed home empty. Even before this the products of the East could no longer be picked up at Constantinople or at Trebizond, for Genghis Khan and his Mongols had destroyed the highway route from China which started westward in the shadow of the great Chinese Wall. Somewhat later another wave of marauders out of Asia, the Ottoman Turks, were to capture Constantinople and to strike deep into Eastern Europe.

In spite of her waning commercial fortunes in the eastern Mediterranean, the greatness of Venice lasted on for another century or more. Her printers were the most influential in Europe; her craftsmen turned out products of continuing excellence. And what was true of Venice was equally true of the great industrial cities of Milan and Florence. But after the year 1600 there were other places whose stars were in the ascendant, places that faced out toward the Atlantic and the New World.

A *Dash of Greek*

We return to the story of the printer. A host of new words, all of them from Greek, came into the English language through the influence of Aldus the printer. They ranged from such printing terms as "typography" and "colophon" to such general ones as "grammar" and "lexicon." Among the words were several that related to Greek punctuation signs. To get some idea as to how such Greek expressions worked into printing practices demands an enlargement of the story of Aldus and his times. In 1453 Constantinople fell before the attacks of the Ottoman Turks. It had been a city of vast wealth and luxury, the final center of Greek culture, the arbiter of Eastern fashions, and the religious center of the Greek Catholic Church. Its capture meant, in particular, the migration of many Greek scholars to Western Europe. In Italy the revival of interest in old writings was already under way. Attention now swung to Greek literature. Greek manuscripts were accumulated; Greek libraries and museums were formed. Greek scholars taught to crowded classes.

In 1490 Aldus set up his press in Venice. He was an enthusiast about Greece. With the aid of Greek scholars and Greek compositors, he had the ancient Greek productions edited for publication in popular editions. From his press came beautifully printed copies of Aristotle, Aristophanes, Thucydides, Sophocles, Herodotus, Demosthenes, and Plutarch. These were printed in Greek. Aldus next turned his attention to the older Latin authors, printing their works in popular editions. He finished with the relatively recent writings of Dante and Erasmus. In all of these book publications the Greek punctuation forms were used. Among the signs so introduced were the colon, comma, hyphen, apostrophe, asterisk, obelus, and parenthesis, as well as the period. Most of them had been in Greek use for centuries. Several had had an interesting history.

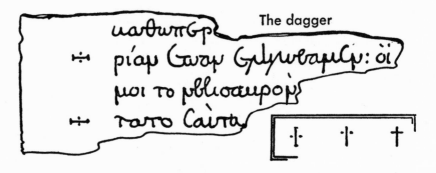

The dagger

The symbol known today as the *"obelisk"* or *"dagger"* started as an *obelus,* "a spit for roasting meat." It was drawn as a short horizontal line with a small cross-line at either end, which is probably what the spit looked like. Then the horizontal line merely had a pair of dots in the center; it looked like our division sign. Next the line with its pair of dots was turned to an up-and-down position. Later the pair of dots slipped toward the upper end of the line. Finally the dots were merged into a short line. By this time the Greek word *obelisk* had taken the place of the Greek word *obelus,* probably by a confusion of ideas. And if you do not fancy Greek names, you call it a dagger, which is what the finished sign resembles.

Asterisk means "star." The asterisk mark of today's press is a nicely designed but simple star picture. The signs of the early Greek manuscripts seem, by contrast, quite crude. A +

sign with dots in the four corners, or an X with those four
dots, was later to be handled as several lines radiating from
a point. Present practice favors a figure with either five or six
radiating arms. But for fifteen centuries there has been no
change of name.

The asterisk

The Greeks had shown an omitted letter by a high comma
that they called an *apostrophe*. In the Latin writings of
Western Europe numerous ways had been used for marking
omissions and abbreviations. Due to the influence of Aldus,
the simple Greek way won out.

Aldus did not use the Greek question mark in his regular
presswork. Or, rather, he did not use it as a question mark.
The writers of Latin had been putting a comma over a dot for
this type of mark. Aldus kept this sign, merely making the
comma extra large. This, the big comma over a small dot, is
the question mark of today.

The question mark

Greek   Latin   English   Spanish

He then changed the Greek question mark of a dot over a comma into a *semi-colon*, a name that he invented.

All of the various Greek marks as introduced by Aldus were to become standard usage among printers and writers, and their Greek names were to become a part of schoolboy language. We might mention, in passing, that one effect among English printers of the adoption of Greek punctuation was to cause the *virgula* to be dropped, its place being taken by the Greek comma. The sloping-line virgula (/) has been kept but given new tasks.

We end this section with a reproduction of the *colophon* of Aldus. The Greek word carried the idea of "end." It was the name of a city in Asia Minor at the dead-end summit of a mountain highway; it was *the end* of the road, or of the printing.

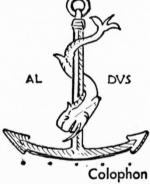

Colophon

Caput and Paragraphus

But not all words of the printer are from the Greek. "Book" was derived from "beech-tree," boards and bark of which were used for early English writing. To "write" meant to "scratch on bark." And to "read" was to "make out," as in solving a riddle. All these terms were from early English.

Certain other words came in from the French, just as they had reached French from Latin. "Pen" was from a French word for "feather," whose quill would be used for writing. "Pencil" carried the old French idea of "little tail," the small tufted brush of the rubricator—which is not the meaning today.

"Head" and "body," as used in writing, referred to the column of written work as the body, the title as the head. The Latin word *caput*, for "head," was widely used in this connection. Through the French came the English expressions of "caption" for the heading, "capitals" for the letter forms of the heading, and "capiter," "chappytre," or "chapter" for the material between headings.

A subdivision of a chapter was often called a *capitulo*, "little chapter." Among English manuscript writers the word

From *caput* to *chapter*

And ze faren yus wiþ zouye sebe freres Wonder me þynkeþ
But Dowel endite zow in þie wdicy ————
Þanne

Capitulo sign of the rubricator

itself was but little used, the sign of a large C, placed in the margin, appearing instead. When inserted by the rubricator, the C would be in color, and the upper swing of the letter would be carried into the written page to mark the division point.

In the hands of the printer the capitulo sign was given a variety of forms and treatment. Some of these are illustrated. In recent forms the C is readily mistaken for a reversed P.

Variety in *capitulo* signs

Today's printer may call the capitulo sign a paragraph sign. But what we might call the "real paragraph sign" would be something quite different. It was an old Greek way of dividing the work upon a page by a line run part of the way across the sheet and joined at the left to a short downward stroke. The Greek word for it was *paragraphus*, "a line drawn."

With us the old Greek sign is quite unnecessary. We have

Greek *paragraphus* sign

too good a substitute. Its story can be started with Alcuin, though Alcuin himself had nothing directly to do with the matter. In preparing for a new section of Bible writing, he had his scribes set an enlarged initial letter somewhat into the margin. After Alcuin's time the rubricators were called upon, more and more, to add color to the handwritten page. The simplest way was to give a more elaborate handling to the initial letters of the sections. And to allow more space for these indulged letters, the book scribe would indent the first three lines or so of the section. The printing press, when it entered the picture, set out to copy exactly the page forms already in use. It printed in black what the book scribes would have written in black, leaving the indented spaces he would have left. As the pages came from the press the sheets would be passed to the rubricator to add the hand-drawn colored initials. But the rubricator could not speed his drawing to the tempo of the press. So the printer came to his aid by having special initial-letter forms designed and cast, to be printed in black along with the rest of the work. This offered a new difficulty. Designs that had been effective in color looked heavy and somber when run in black. The situation was helped by simpler and smaller designs. But for some odd reason the in-dented spaces were left as before, making the new initials look strangely shrunken in their big spaces.

In today's presswork the initial is often back to the com-parative size of Alcuin's time. But it is not placed where Alcuin had it. It is now set away from the margin a few type spaces. And today not only the sectional divisions are treated in this way. Even the shortest paragraph has its own in-dented line to mark its beginning. Such things are now stand-ard practice. But occasionally one may find some printers or some writers experimenting with ways of breaking up the steady marshaling of lines upon the page other than by the use of indented spaces. They are getting some interesting results.

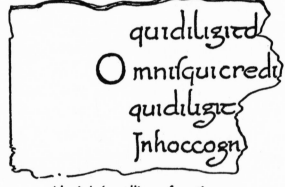

Alcuin's handling of sections

Hitting the Keys

Printing was wonderful. But the work of the printer was laborious. The setting of type by hand was not particularly difficult, but it was painstakingly slow. Letter by letter the type would be picked up and placed in position—going from right to left, so that the printed line would read from left to right. Space bars would be inserted to make the last letter of the line come at the exact place the other lines ended—and so on. Then would come the press work. At the job's end the letters would have to be loosened from the printing frames, then dropped, one by one, each into its own compartment, ready for the next run.

The wider use of printing awaited the development of something less laborious. Ottmar Mergenthaler came to the rescue with a machine so complete but so complicated that the officials of the United States Patent Office had to see the machine in operation before they believed that the idea would work. He got his patents. The Mergenthaler device is called a *linotype machine*. The operator plays upon the keyboard, setting about 500 inches of type an hour. As he presses each key on the keyboard in front of him the matrix of that letter will fall from a magazine to its proper place in the line—the matrix being a mold with the letter form indented in it. After each word he touches a space key. That inserts a steel space band having two wedge-shaped parts. At the line's end a handle is thrown. An electric motor sets the machine to work to change the line into permanent type, while the operator can go to work immediately on the next line. In its almost uncanny way the machine moves the line of matrices into a boxlike mold; the wedges of the space bands are pushed in just enough to bring the line to the wanted length. Melted casting metal then floods the mold to the brim. Upon cooling, this leaves a solid "line-o'-type." After that the matrices are quickly unscrambled, and the letters travel up a channel to the top of the device. Each matrix drops through a hole into its own special magazine compartment, for it carries a "key" to that one entering-space.

But why run along with your imagination in understanding the workings of the linotype machine? It is so easy to see the device at work. Look in at your newspaper printing shop. You can hear the matrices as they drop, see the finished lines of type still warm from the melted metal, and watch the row of matrices move steadily to the top and then drop through the proper holes. Other typesetting machines have been invented also. And the use of them all, with the great automatic presses of today to speed the type into print, has been an important factor in bringing the printed word to everyone's door.

We should not leave unmentioned a low-priced, portable printing device designed for office or home use. The operator sits before a simple keyboard. As the key is pressed, up flies the type, printing as it strikes. Then down the type drops until wanted again. It is no real substitute for the printing press. By itself it can make but one direct print. The lines do not end up automatically of the same length. The work does not have the appearance of presswork; narrow i is given the same space-width as wide m. As you will have known instantly, this machine is the *typewriter*. To be sure, the inventors could have built the typewriter to a different pattern. They could have had an arrangement for bringing the lines to an even end, as in presswork; they could have given presswork sizes to the various letters. But who would buy a machine so designed, for office or home use? Not I. I can now correct the error of a single letter on a typed page without retyping the whole line that the letter is in. The letter that I should have put in will have the same space-width as the one

I used. And the typewriter of today can make a number of copies with carbon paper. And the typed page can be turned over to the printer, if desired, for regular reproduction by the offset printing process. It is a clever thing, this typewriter.

CHAPTER **9**

Secretaries
& Signs

That Fine Italian Hand

Our comments about the typewriter should remind us
that nothing as yet has been said about the job of the secretary and about handwritten letters. We should rectify this
situation, for handwriting has had its styles as well as manuscript writing. And many of the odd written signs of the
business office have come from the writing shortcuts of secretary and clerk.

Alfred the Great, King of Saxon England, needed no secretary. He was well versed in Latin, the diplomatic language of
the time, could write fluently in Anglo-Saxon, and was an able
penman. But others who followed him—the kings and queens
and high officials of England—had an almost constant need
for someone with learning who could handle the messages of
diplomacy and the correspondence of daily life. They were
able men, these secretaries of royalty and nobility.

Many official written documents on parchment have come
down to us from the period that followed the time of Alfred.
Certain things seem notable about these writings of the
secretaries. They seldom show the almost machine-like strokes

116

*.(M). impatrix h).reg filia 7 anglox dña Baronib'Juft
miniftriS. 7 omĩb; fidelib° ruiS franciS 7 angliS de kent fat*

*The grant by the Empress Matilda to Christ Church in 1141
represents a good example of the penmanship of that time. The
written material is full of abbreviations, as may be seen by comparing the full text with the written copy.*

   *M(atilda) imperatrix H(enrici) regis filia et anglorum domina
      Baronibus Just.*
   *ministris et omnibus fidelibus suis francis et anglis de kent
      salutem*

of the trained book scribe. There is originality, a sort of
"verve," an impression of studied informality. Peculiarities
of word handling are shown by a clustering of letters into
groups. Abbreviations are frequent, with few set rules, apparently.

In the days of the black letters English secretaries shifted
over to the use of the broad-nibbed pen. And when the book
scribes added an excessive ornamentation, the secretaries did
the same thing. You can imagine the result—a combination
of illegible writing and confusing abbreviations! Maybe the
secretaries could not make out their own writing and what it
meant when it "got cold."

In 1430 Joan of Arc was leading the soldiers of France in
driving the English forces out of her country. England itself
was approaching a time of civil war known to history as the
War of the Roses. In sixty-two years Columbus would be
sailing west toward a new world. In that year of 1430 Niccolo
di Niccoli, official clerk of the Vatican at Rome, was devising

for himself a new handwriting script. Now this was the time
of the Italian revival of interest in old books and the shifting
of book-scribe writing from black-letter forms to the old letter
forms of Alcuin. Niccolo was a creative artist, not a mere
copyist. Taking the English forms of handwritten letters of
1200 as his models, he built about them a new script. He
changed the letter shapes slightly so that all the letters of a
word could be written without lifting the pen before the end
of the word was reached. In addition to this, vertical strokes
of the letters were given loops at the bottom or top. A slight
slant was given to the letter strokes also, which gave distinc-
tion. You will note what he was after: rapidity, legibility, dis-
tinction. He met them all.

It is not often that the handwriting of a single person can
change that of a nation. Niccolo's did more than that. As
clerk of the Vatican he handled a large amount of official
correspondence that went out to the leading churchmen of
Europe. Their clerks, in turn, copied Niccolo's handwriting
style, calling it the *Italian hand*. After that, individuals
adopted it for their own personal correspondence. Aldus the
printer had these script letters cut in a type form that he was
to name *italics*. Eventually men in business adopted the script
for office use. Finally it reached the public schools; everyone
wanted to write with that "fine Italian hand." And the penmanship taught in your school is of the Niccolo kind!

Niccolo's writing was planned for paper, not for parchment.
It discouraged the use of abbreviations, since the rapidity of
the new manner of writing and the low cost of paper no longer
demanded an extreme economy of time and material. It was
aimed at uniformity. But the writers who, in the past three

El vizcayno lo
1548
Penmanship

Lettre carreé commune
1651

When an humour is strong
1618

If you not new
1712

centuries, have followed his penmanship styles have never
lacked opportunity to show their own individuality.

Ergo and Videlicet

The story now shifts briefly to the law clerks of England
and to the queer abbreviations that they and the lawyers have
passed down to us.

Latin was for a long time the official language of the law
courts of England. All legal documents were written in Latin
words. That situation changed centuries ago. And one would
suppose that today there would be nothing left from those
old Latin days. But many a lawyer still seeks to impress a
courtroom audience and a jury with Latin phrases, and many
a clerk, following custom, garnishes the legal papers he is
preparing with old Latin abbreviations.

Here are some you may have seen in either legal or general
publications. (The periods are not put in, which gives the
abbreviation its original form.)

Is Newton
1682

Ben Jonson
1647

Galileo Galilei
1609

Voltaire
1760

Franklin
1784

michelagniolo
1508

Penmanship

i e (that is)   *e g* (for example)   *c* (about)

ad fin (at the end)   *ad lib* (at liberty or at pleasure)

ad loc (at the place)   *et al* (and others)

etc (and other things)   *et seq* (and the following)

ibid (in the same place)   *loq* (he speaks)

n b (note well)   *ob* (he died)   *per an* (by the year)

nol pros (to be unwilling to prosecute)   *vs* (against)

non seq (it does not follow)   *pro tem* (for the time being)

prox (in the coming month)

One word of the legal Latin was seldom abbreviated: *ergo* (therefore). Another received an unexpectedly queer abbreviation by having an old sign of abbreviation taken for a hastily written z. This was the word *videlicet* (namely), which ended up as viz.

The "penner-and-inkhorn" attached to this English clerk's belt was the earlier substitute for the present-day fountain pen. The pen, of course, was but a goose quill cut to a point with a "pen-knife."

Word Signs from the Counting Houses

A typewriter in today's business office is apt to carry upon the keyboard some queer signs that had their beginning in the days when business establishments were known as *counting houses* and Italian expressions were in common use. For that was the time when Venice, Milan, Florence, and Genoa were the greatest business cities of them all.

The words "box," "bench," and "fee" are English; "cash," "bank," and "money" are from the Italian. "Hatter" is English; "milliner" is Italian. The last had its word beginning as "Milaner," the shop of a Milan-born dealer in men's hats. But more important to our story than the Italian business words themselves are the odd signs and the peculiar abbreviations the English clerks picked up from the Italian business houses. Strangely enough, these signs and abbreviations, now almost meaningless in themselves, are features of today's business reports just as they have been for centuries.

People of today have wondered why our word "number" carries the strange abbreviation of "No." The Italians are responsible for that. "N°" was their abbreviation for *numero,* a word frequently used in business orders that meant "in number" or "to the number of." For half a thousand years this old, foreign letter-combination has remained in current English use. We do, however, give the old term a somewhat distorted meaning when we say "Table No. 2" and mean the *second* table. The Italians would not have used *numero* in that way.

The Italian word *ditto* was another expression in wide business use. It meant "the aforesaid" or "that which has been mentioned." It was used in referring to a month previously mentioned or, in a general way, to avoid tedious repetitions of any sort. The clerk's abbreviation for the word was d°, a letter combination which when written small and rapidly came to resemble a reversed comma followed by a period. The comma-and-dot arrangement, not recognized as a letter combination, was to lead later clerks to use such variations as a pair of inverted commas, a pair of ordinary commas or a pair of dots as the *ditto* sign.

Ditto

The sign or symbol for "per cent" got its start in the Italian business houses. The original expression, for which the sign came to be used, was *numero per cento*, which, being interpreted, reads "to this number in a hundred." The earliest form of the abbreviation probably had N° for the first part of the expression, a sloping line for the "per" and a C for the idea of 100. Later the carelessly written C appeared as the letter O, and the sign as we know it came into existence, the N of the N° being lost.

The English handling of the *numero per cento* expression

Per cent

went through as many changes, perhaps, as the sign itself. Always shortened in some way, it appeared at first, according to the Oxford English Dictionary, as *per cento* or *per cent*. About 1650 the use of *per centum* became the vogue. This seemed to give a Latin appearance to the expression, though no correct Latin phrase would have had this form. This particular spelling of *per centum* and its abbreviated form of *per cent.*, with its period, have continued in English use to some extent. More recently "percent" as a word, not an abbreviation, has been gaining ground.

The sign & is quite correctly read "and," for it is only a peculiar handling of *et*, the word for "and" in Latin, Italian, French, and other Western European languages. Early forms used by the book scribe and clerk show the e and t quite clearly, joined as a letter combination. More recent shapes given to the sign range from an evident *et* to a scroll form in which the letters seem unrecognizable.

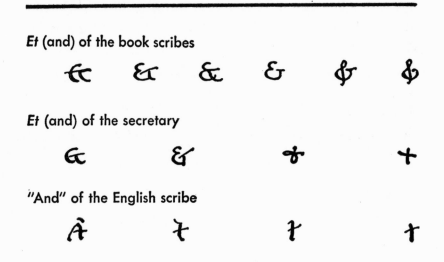

Et (and) of the book scribes

Et (and) of the secretary

"And" of the English scribe

The English have called this sign of & an *ampersand*. According to the Oxford English Dictionary, which carries a wealth of information on old word-usage, the word was a compression of a half-English, half-Latin expression "and per se—and." This was a way of saying that the sign itself and with nothing added represented the word "and."

The + sign of arithmetic may have started as a form of *et*. It may, instead, have come from a quick-written way of handling the English word "and." A third possibility is that it was derived from the Italian abbreviation for the word *plus*, which in business houses meant "more." Intermediate forms taken from secretarial writings would suggest as quite plausible that the forms for all three of the suggested origins were converging toward the form used today.

There is more certainty about the beginnings of the subtraction sign (—). The Italian and Latin word *minus*, meaning "less," was used in marking packages that were short in weight. As an abbreviation, the letter M was put on the package with a line over it. It is entirely probable that this M-and-line combination, with the letter omitted, gave us the present-day minus sign.

Plus (more)

$$\widehat{P} \qquad P \qquad \mp \qquad +$$

Minus (less)

$$\widehat{M} \qquad \overline{m} \qquad \overline{m} \qquad -$$

The sign @ used in a business with the meaning "at the rate of" was originally ā, the line over the letter indicating abbreviation. The full word was *ana*, "treating all alike." The secretarial scribe and the clerk ran the letter and line together, without lifting the pen from the paper in doing so, to get the present form of the sign.

When the first letter of an abbreviated word was tall, it was the custom of that time to draw a line, showing abbreviation, across the vertical part of the letter rather than above it. Such a plan was used by the Italians with their word *recipe*, meaning "take." In prescriptions the abbreviation for *recipe* would be followed by a statement as to the quantities of drugs to be compounded. The abbreviation itself was a capital R with the line of abbreviation drawn diagonally across the letter, giving the familiar ℞ (which some have thought was short for "Rex").

The Italian *libbra* (from the old Latin word *libra*, "balance") represented a weight almost exactly equal to the avoirdupois pound of England. The Italian abbreviation of *lb* with a line for abbreviation drawn across the letters was, in general business dealings, used for both weights. The business clerk's hurried way of writing the abbreviation appears to have been responsible for the # sign used for "pound."

Pound weight

℔   ℔   ℔   #

The Sign of the Dollar

There is one sign on the typewriter keyboard for which the Italians were not responsible. That is the sign of the dollar. So in closing our brief handling of the queer signs of business we shall need to slip in the story of the $ sign.

In the year 1519 a large silver coin was minted for the first time at Joachimsthal in Bohemia. This piece of unusual size, produced in large and steady quantities, was officially a *gulden*. In trade usage it was, more often, a *Joachsthaler*; or, shortened, a *thaler*, a *dahler*, a *daler* or a *dollar*. Its minting set a new style in coin-making. Denmark put out a *rigsdaler*, Sweden a *riksdaler*. Spain followed with a coin minted in the West Indies that was to become widely known as the *Spanish dollar*. That was not its official name. To the Spanish it was a *peso de plata*, or "piece of silver." To the Americans it was a "piece-of-eight," for the *peso* was equal in value to 8 Spanish *reals*.

The *peso* as a silver coin was minted in large quantities and was far better known to the American colonists than the British shilling. When the time came for the United States as a new country to have a coinage system of its own, the name of "dollar" was suggested for the new coin, the weight

Origin of the dollar sign

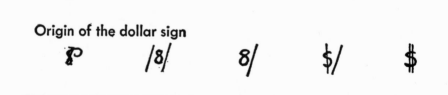

and size to be modeled after those of the *peso*. This suggestion was officially adopted. So the word "dollar," the nickname of a foreign coin, became the official name for one of our own.

The symbol that we use for the dollar was already in use for the Spanish peso. John Fitzpatrick, writing about "The Spanish Galleon and Pieces-of-Eight" in the November 1907 issue of *Scribner's Magazine*, traces the history of the symbol. In its first form it had been a P and 8 blended by a continuous stroking of the pen. Later the P was omitted and the 8 bordered on each side by a sloping line. Eventually the pair of lines was superimposed on the 8. In the next step the 8, by careless writing, was to appear as S. In $, its final form, there was sufficient resemblance to a U and S woven together to make the symbol an unusually appropriate one for the standard of United States coinage.

On this comparatively modern level we leave the story of the origin of our signs. It is essentially a tale that can never be complete. New signs and symbols will come into use; older ones may slowly be discarded. But how very persistent the old forms have been—too persistent, perhaps.

The Number Symbols

Gobar Numerals

We have left for discussion a group of keyboard symbols that we call the numerals. We call them Arabic, but they were not invented by the Arabians. The Arabic scholars called them Persian numerals, but they were not invented by the Persians. The Persian scholars referred to them as Hindu symbols. They were right, for the original number symbols had been invented in India and used by the Hindu scholars, along with a counting-by-ten number plan and a calculating device made of beads on wires, known to us as an *abacus*.

It seems quite probable that the original shapes of the Hindu numerals had followed a simple but unusual tally-mark way of handling. The four, for example, had apparently been merely four short lines built into a simple square. The eight had its eight short lines forming two squares that

---

Hindu numbers (conjectured)

—	=	≡	⊐	Ⴆ	ⴹ	ⴼ	ⴽ	ⴾ	·
1	2	3	4	5	6	7	8	9	0

touched at a corner. In the sketch below you can see how the other numerals had their shapes worked out in a similar way, each figure having as many short-line strokes as its number value.

It is easy to see why this manner of handling would have been used in the first place. In India the writing of messages has long been done with a dull-pointed stylus that makes indented marks on the surface of a dried palm leaf. The small spaces between the ribs of the leaf and the difficulty in handling curves on such a surface would make that writing easiest which would use short straight lines and combine them into simple figures.

The construction plan seems simple: each numeral made from the number of strokes that it was to represent. We should hasten to state, however, that no ancient example of such a palm-indented record has ever been found. This lack of evidence is, of course, not strange. Dried palm leaves might be expected to crumble into dust long before even a century had passed. And the plan itself may date back fifteen centuries or more. The earliest known Hindu numeral record is not nearly that old. It is a rock-cut inscription, and on it the severely simple straight-sided figures do not appear.

The Hindu number-symbols would, without a doubt, have been of no special importance had they not been used with a calculation plan, invented by the Hindu scholars, that had outstanding value. It was this plan that was passed on from one scholarly group to another; the number symbols went along with the plan. And in this passage from group to group some changes in number shape occurred. These changes were not deliberate; they merely reflected the nature of the writing medium and the stylus or pen used with it. The Persians wrote on parchment with a pen. Straight lines with them changed to curves; the tally marks of the two and of the three were run together into a continuous figure; the seven was greatly simplified. In the hands of the Arabic scholars only one major change was made. The number forms were reversed; for the Arabians wrote on parchment or paper in Phoenician style, from right to left.

Form changes of the "Arabic" number symbols

Hindu (conjectured)	—	=	≡	⊐	৬	5	日	⅁	믱	
Early forms	—	Z	≢	⊿	৬	৳	Ȝ	8	9	o
	ı	Z	∃	⊐	ঢ	৬	ɔ	8	9	ø
Gobar forms (reversed)	ı	Z	3	Ȣ	ʔ	6	∧	8	9	o
	ı	2	3	Ȣ	5	6	7	8	9	o
Italian of 1500	ı	2	3	4	5	6	7	8	9	o

The number plan reached the Arabic scholars at a time of a great advance in mathematics. They had invented algebra; they called it *el-gebr*. Complex arithmetic problems were being handled; they called them *algorism*. The present way of writing common fractions was their invention. A beginning toward using logarithms had been made. And in natural science the laws of the reflection and refraction of light had been worked out. Somewhat before the year 1000 the new mathematics, which could be so helpful to the scholar in predicting the heights of coming tides, the time of solar and lunar eclipses, and the length of earth meridians, had worked westward. Passed from one scholarly group to another, it had reached the schools of northern Africa and the great Moorish universities of Moslem Spain.

Another development was also under way that used the Hindu calculation plan. In the Arabic schools of northern Africa the plan and the numerals used with it were being put to work in the computations of business. In these schools the number symbols were referred to as *gobar* numbers, from an Arabic word for "dust." It has been surmised that the name came from the black wood tablets covered with a sprinkling of chalky dust that could substitute for the earlier

1	2	3	4	5	6	7	8	9	10
2	4	6	8	10	12	14	16	18	20
3	6	9	12	15	18	21	24	27	30
4	8	12	16	20	24	28	32	36	40
5	10	15	20	25	30	35	40	45	50
6	12	18	24	30	36	42	48	54	60
7	14	21	28	35	42	49	56	63	70
8	16	24	32	40	48	56	64	72	80
9	18	27	30	45	54	63	72	81	90
10	20	30	40	50	60	70	80	90	100

This multiplication table, from John of Holywood's Algorismus, *was printed from an engraved plate. The present forms of the 4, 5, and 7 are quite changed in appearance from these reversed-Gobar numbers.*

black wax tablets. Lines drawn in the dust would show up as black marks. (But any sudden gust of wind might blow away a whole arithmetic exercise.)

In Western Europe only Spain was a Moslem country in the days of which we have been writing. And Christian Europe knew only by hearsay about the new number plan and the number symbols used with it. Eventually a few scholars from France were to apply for admission to the great Moorish universities of Spain, there to gain a first-hand knowledge of the new mathematics and the new approach to natural science. And about the same time Leonardo Fibonacci, son of an Italian merchant who as a buyer of Moslem goods was located for a time in northern Africa, went to a Moslem business school.

Leonardo grew up. He became a merchant of Pisa in Italy. And, being trained in the new mathematics, he used the gobar numbers in problems of buying and selling—problems that no Italian businessman of the time could possibly have solved by the old Roman number plan. Eventually he put down in Italian words the things he had learned in the Arabic school, which he wanted other businessmen to know. He completed his manuscript in the year 1202. In putting down the gobar number symbols, he reversed their direction, for the Italians wrote from left to right. And almost at the same time a French scholar, trained in Spain, was completing his scholarly treatise on the new mathematics. He too reversed the gobar numerals.

From these two handwritten manuscripts, passed around and copied, the new knowledge slowly spread; in Italy to those interested in business, in France and England to the scholars. Eventually the spreading of this knowledge was hastened by the efforts of the early printers. Copies of the Arabic form of the multiplication table, with brief directions for its use, were run off from engraved plates. A half-century later regularly printed books went on sale that gave full directions on how to handle the "Arabic" numbers in multiplication and division and business accounts. All the larger merchant cities of Germany, Flanders, and Holland had by this time put in special schools for teaching the new calculation methods. The production of self-help arithmetics for these schools was a boon to the early printers. In another century the common schools of Western Europe would be teaching the new methods of arithmetic that made use of the "Arabic" numerals.

In the two manuscripts that gave the original introduction of the so-called Arabic numbers to Christian Europe the reversed gobar symbols were essentially alike. In the three centuries that followed, some changes of form crept in. This result came from the writing habits of the Italian business secretaries and clerks. When printing from movable type came into the picture it was the forms of the Italian business office that were followed by Jenson and Aldus. In their type the numeral 1 was hard to distinguish from minuscule l; numeral 6 was merely an inverted 9. (Or is it the other way?)

Aldus died about four centuries ago. Since that time the business clerks of America, in particular, have developed for themselves an unadorned numeral *1*, a more open *4*, and a distinctive *9*. These better symbols are taught in today's schoolrooms. But many printers have stayed close to the old Italian forms of centuries ago. And the typewriter-makers

seem to have taken a backward step in using the minuscule l
for the numeral 1, just to save half a key space on the machine.

Nothing has been said up to this point about the numeral
0, so readily mistaken today for a capital O. On that early
rock-cut Hindu inscription a dot had been used. Persian
scholars had replaced the dot by a more conspicuous symbol,
that of 0. To the Arabic scholars this symbol was *sifr*.
Fibonacci, in writing for the Italians, lengthened the word to
zephirum. Two centuries later the Italian clerks were calling
it *zeuero*; still later it was *zero*. Among the French the Arabic
sifr was given the French spelling of *cyffre*. The English put
it down as *sipher* or *cipher*. And that is how the name of the
symbol ended up in English as two different words, *zero* and
cipher. When we call the symbol by the still different name
of *naught* ("nothing") we are adding an idea not found in
the original plan.

*Al Khowarazmi, Arabic mathematician
and writer.*

The Ways of Roman Numbers

The Romans used letters, not special numeral figures, in their way of recording numbers. Thus they would write out such a number as 1956 with the letter combination MDCCCCLVI. As this represents a peculiar use of letters, we may wonder how such a plan was started and how it worked.

The Phoenicians began the plan of using alphabet letters in number-writing. Thus 'aleph, their first letter, not only represented a letter sound but also was used for the number one. *Beth*, the second letter, was used also for the number two. Put into our letters, their number plan ran like this:

1	2	3	4	5	6	7	8	9	10
A	B	C	D	E	F	G	H	I	J

11	12	13	14	15	16	17	18	19	20
JA	JB	JC	JD	JE	JF	JG	JH	JI	K

21	22	23 . . . 29	30	31 . . . 40 . . . 50 . . . 60 . . . 100
KA	KB	KC . . . KI	L	LA . . . M . . . N . . . O . . . S

They had 22 letters. The first 9 of these were for the digits from 1 to 9. The next 9 were for 10, 20, 30, on up to 90. That left 4 letters; these were used for 100, 200, 300 and 400. The counting plan thus ran to 499. Counting started over again at that point (500).

The Greeks took over the Phoenician number plan along with their alphabet. We know that this is true because two very early Greek letters got into the number plan but were later dropped out of the alphabet. These were *digamma*, used for 6, and *koppa*, for 90. Eventually the classical Greek alphabet carried four additional letters. In the number plan these were used for 500, 600, 700, and 800. The Greeks needed one more. They got it by turning the *psi* symbol upside down. In this extended way, the plan ran to 999. At 1000 they started over. For really large numbers the later Greek philosophers used an accent mark by the side of a letter to give it a value 1000 times its usual value. Thus A' V R B by the Greek plan but using our letters would be for the number 1 thousand 4 hundred 92 (or 1492).

We might suppose that the Romans would have used the Greek style of number plan. They got their ways of doing things in nearly all cases from the Etruscans, and the Etruscans used an old Greek letter plan for numbers. But the Romans seem to have been sidetracked. They ended up with a part of the Etruscan plan mixed in with a tally-recording scheme of their own. You may have seen that old Roman tally plan in use in recording the votes at election time. It is a counting-by-five arrangement. Strokes are made for the first four counts, a diagonal line is marked across the four strokes for the fifth count. The Romans used crossing diagonals for the tenth stroke. To record the result of a count, each 10 was shown by an X; an additional 5 would appear as a V; each ad-

Roman numbers

Tally	I	II	III	IIII	ℕ	ℕI	ℕII	ℕIII	ℕIIII	ℕ⋈
Number	I	II	III	IIII	V	VI	VII	VIII	VIIII	X

ditional stroke less than 5 appeared as I. In the line drawing, you can see why they put V for 5.

For the larger number of their counting-by-five procedure

Roman symbols for large numbers

	Etruscan	Roman		
50	↓	↓	⊥	L
100	⊙	⊙	O	C
1000	Φ	(I)	ⅭⅮ	M
500		Ɑ or D	D	

the Romans took some Etruscan symbols that had been left out in developing the Latin alphabet. These were used for 50, 100, and 1000. The idea was probably good enough. But these particular forms, having no use as letters, developed into variant shapes. Finally the old sign for 50 was rather deliberately made into an L, while that for 100 ended up as C and the one for 1000 as M. In the last two cases the letters were quite appropriate. The Latin word for 100 was *centum*, starting with C; that for 1000 was *mille*, starting with M. The Roman use of D for 500 has been explained as a splitting in half of the old symbol for 1000 and the use of the right half, which looked much like D, as the symbol for half of 1000. Incidentally, the use of IV for 4 and IX for 9 did not come in Roman times but about a thousand years later.

The use of Roman numbers in calculations was normally quite awkward. For example, it took 9 figures to give the

Roman number for 1956, which could be expressed with less than half that many figures in either the Greek or Arabic plans. Actually calculations were not made in Roman numbers from the written-down figures as they are today. A special adding machine had to be brought into use—again the *abacus*. In its earliest form the device was a flat piece of wood with grooves cut in its surface, each groove long enough to hold five pebbles. Adding would be done by filling the grooves one by one and then counting up the totals by fives or tens. In the time of the Empire an improved form was available. Fewer pebbles were needed, and the adding was completed more rapidly. Multiplication was handled by repeated additions. (If the problem was to multiply 122 by 5 the abacus would be used to count 122 pebbles, added on to 122 pebbles, added on to 122 pebbles, added on to 122 pebbles, added on to 122 pebbles, all of which was rather tiresome.) Division could be handled only by guesswork. As the Roman word for pebble was *calculus*, they "calculated" when they used the pebbles for problem work.

The abacus remained in use long after Roman times. In Western Europe its form changed with the centuries until all that remained of the original idea might be a group of grooves cut into the top of the shelf where goods would be sold, with a dish or sack of small shells for the counting. By that time the original name of *abacus* had long been forgotten. It was merely a *counter*. And, today, the "counter" is the shelf, from which the grooves have been missing for two centuries.

Signs Peculiar to Music

Disguised Letters

Business has had its signs that started out as quickly written letters and ended up as nearly unintelligible designs. These have been discussed. Written music has had its signs, too, that once represented something quite understandable.

Most of the signs and marks on today's written music had their beginning as letters, hooks, curves, dots, and dashes. They resulted from the attempt, a thousand years ago, to guide a singer through a song. The excessive vagueness of the first efforts was gradually replaced by something quite definite. The story of the signs of music is quite largely, then, a record of the efforts of the musician to develop a sure guide for the singer.

The dots and dashes were in the beginning placed high above the words for high tones and less high for tones not so high. The plan seems reasonable. But there was nothing at first to show *how* high each word should be sung. True, the stringed instruments of that day could be used to sound the scale for the singers and to start them off on a tone pitch of F or C, or some other tone value. The trouble was that the

139

music did not show where the F or C would be needed. This situation, however, was definitely helped when a thoughtful scribe drew a red line across the page above the words to divide the marks intended for tones above F from those below F. Additional help was furnished by a second scribe who added a yellow line across the page, above the red one, to take care of the tone of C. After that other lines went in, drawn in black. There were the A-line, the E-line, and so on. The spaces between the lines were used for half the tones of the octave and the lines themselves for the other half, which is the way the matter has been handled ever since.

After the red and yellow lines had been in use for about two centuries, the use of color was dropped, and these lines, like the rest, were drawn in black. The letter F or the letter C, at the beginning of the line, was used instead of color. The F and the C would not both be put on a sheet of music; one of them was enough. At that time song parts for men with low voices were written on a group of lines in which the F line would be the one next to the top, this line being marked with an F. This group of lines came to be known as the *bass* or *basso* clef, since *bass* (French) and *basso* (Italian) meant "low." For men with higher voices the group of lines ran higher, with the C line marked by the letter. This group was the *alto* clef. *Alto* (Italian) meant "high." (Today that same clef can be used for women with low voices, so an alto singer is a woman with a low voice, not a high one.) When church song parts began to be written for women, a third clef came into use that had the G line marked. It was the *treble* clef—meaning "third."

For some time the letters used for clef signs were kept

small and drawn in a simple way. But when all writing became more elaborate, as happened in the days of the black
letters, the letters of the clef signs became more elaborate
also. Eventually they were as large as the staff of five lines,
and embellished with fancy strokes and flourishes. It is these
over-embellished letters that are to be found on the music
page of today. One can scarcely believe that the sign of the
treble clef, for example, is intended for a G; it does not look
that way. But the G-line passes through the widest part of the
sign, just as it did when the letter was simple. And the F
of the bass clef looks strangely unlike a letter. A pair of dots
have taken the place of the bar of the F. And the F-line of the
music passes between the dots, just as it used to pass through

Clef sign changes

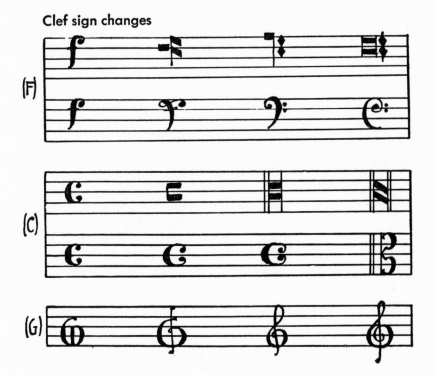

the bar. And the C of the clef used for high voices with men or low voices with women is quite as difficult to interpret, unless you know that it too is a letter in disguise—and the disguise is almost bafflingly perfect.

Before the day of presswork there would ordinarily be but one large sheet of the music prepared for the men with low voices, and the words would be large enough for all to see. Another large sheet would be made for the women singers. After the printing press made duplication easy it was often more convenient to have the parts for men and women on the same sheet, with many copies made. Only the staffs of the F and G clefs might then be given, the C-line, otherwise unmarked, being drawn in color between the marked staffs. The words had to be placed either above or below the rest. Later the F and G staffs were separated and the words set between them, as is today's custom. This change left the C-line in the peculiar position of being above one staff and below the other; it was "middle C."

And now for the story of how our notes came to be.

In the beginning the notes of today were accent marks. Thus a simple accent stroke was used for a high note. After staff lines came into use this mark, with a widened head, was placed on the scale at the point that would match its tone

Virga (accent)

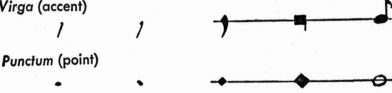

/   1

Punctum (point)

.   .

value. In black-letter days this accent mark, as drawn with a wide-nibbed pen, had a conspicuous appearance on the music page, the head being broad and the tail a thin-edged stroke. This made it look like a "real note," as we would say. The other mark, keeping up with the accent mark in its changes, was the *punctum*, or "point," used originally for a low note. By the twelfth century it had grown from a big dot or period into a small lozenge-shaped figure, as drawn with the flat stroke of a wide-nibbed pen. It too had begun to look like a "real note."

By this time the idea of using the accent type of note for high tones and the point type for low tones had been replaced by another idea, that of letting the notes show how long the tone would be held. The tailed accent note took care of tones of short duration, the lozenge-shaped point note was to handle the tones that were to be held longer. For still shorter tones the tails had pennants hung on them; for still longer tones the lozenges were made white by showing merely an ink border. Among the Italian music scribes the swing away from the black-letter styles and the dropping of the wide-nibbed pen were to result in the oval notes that are used today. And to those scribes and the music lovers of Italy we are indebted for such words of the music page as *allegro moderato, crescendo, piano, solo, forte, tempo di valse, a tempo, coda, dolce, del signo, andante religioso, piu mosso, lento, allegretto, poco meno mosso, con grazia,* and so on.

The clef signs are not the only musical signs that once were letters. The sign of the flat (♭) was a letter. It was a black-letter form of minuscule b. Placed on the B-line, it was to show that the tone of the B was being softened, or lowered a half-tone. The same sign was used later for any staff note that was to be lowered a half-tone. When, in the music, the B-tone was to be restored, the old order was to be canceled out by a lattice of crossed lines. This crossed-out sign is now called a sharp (♯), by contrast with the idea of flat.

We close this part of the history of musical writing by picturing a portion of the oldest existing English song manuscript. It has a six-line staff, with the C-line marked. The words are those of Chaucer, and the music was written as a two-part rondel for men's voices. It is the work of an English monk about the year 1240. In more modern wording, the first line reads:

Summer is a-coming in; loud sings (the) cuckoo . . .

Old song to Chaucer's words

The Do, Re, Mi's

It is true that the origin of the *do, re, mi*'s of the singing classes has really nothing to do with our subject of letters, numbers, and signs. But we might slip the story in to help make the tale more complete. Long before the use of notes had taken form on the music page, monks were singing their religious songs to a scale of *ut-re-mi-fa-sol-la-sa-io*, pronounced in true Latin style. This plan is credited to Guido, a famous singing-master who lived two centuries after Alcuin and Charlemagne. In training a new group, he would start with an old Latin chant to Saint John. This was a good one to use, for the different phrases of the chant began on tones that went regularly up the scale. Guido would have his singers go through the chant over and over, putting emphasis upon the first syllable of each phrase, for it was these particular syllables that held the tones of the scale. He might then have them practice the singing of *re-fa-re, ut-mi-sol,* or any other group of tones. When the time came for a new song to be re-hearsed it would be learned in terms of *ut-re-mi's,* and the use of the real words came later.

Guido has been dead for nine hundred years. But the singing methods that he used and most of the syllables of the old chant to Saint John are still the treasured possessions of the music teachers of Europe and America. It is true that the teachers of England and the United States have changed both the first and last tones of the scale to the word *do,* while the teachers of France use *ut* for the first and *do* for the last. But it has never seemed desirable to any of them, English or French, to substitute something more recent than the

Latin of Guido's day. And that is remarkable. (Given below are the words for the chant, with the first syllables of each line forming the singing scale.)

Ut queant laxis
Re·fonare Fibris
Mi·ra geftorum
Fa·muli tuorum
Sol·ue polluti
La·bij reatum
Sanc· te
Jo·hannes

Hymn to Saint John

CHAPTER I 2

Non-Roman Alphabets

I once had a typewriter that could do tricks. I could get it to write correspondence and messages in Greek or in He-brew. I think it might have handled Arabic, had I wished it, or even Russian. You may have seen a machine like it. The typing was done from a half-circle band of metal that carried on its face the type for a full list of letters and symbols. Strike some key on the keyboard, and the type-band would rotate quickly just the proper amount; then the mechanism would rock forward and the type would hit the ribbon and print the letter on the writing paper. When you released the key, the type-band would spin back to its starting point. The operation could be annoyingly slow for a speedy typist. But the results would be pleasing to one, like myself, looking for variety in typing work. I had several type-bands from which to choose, and one could be substituted for another in a matter of seconds.

With a typewriter having such capabilities I have found it possible to get a quick acquaintance with the alphabets of other lands. I am proposing, then, a brief excursion into the realm of four non-Roman alphabets of the present day.

The Hebrew Alphabet

The typewriter I have been describing is awkward about Hebrew writing. It wants to write from the left side of the paper to the right; Hebrew writing goes the other way. I could, however, get the machine to inch slowly backward across the page by pressing the back-space key twice after every letter key I hit. That makes the job unusually slow. But Hebrew writing puts in only the consonants, so the matter of typing need not take too long—if one remembers about the back-space key.

Now for a little hurried history. The earliest Hebrew letters were exactly like those of the Phoenicians. And the letters had like names, though the *gamal* of the Phoenicians was pronounced *gimel* by the Hebrews. A national calamity in the year 586 B.C. set the stage for a new era that affected writing styles as it did other, more political, things. In that year Nebuchadrezzar of Babylon captured Jerusalem and carried off to the Euphrates Valley a major portion of those who survived the fall of the city. About fifty years later Babylon itself was sacked by the Medes and Persians under Cyrus. A patriotic remnant of the Hebrews was, in time, permitted to return to Jerusalem and rebuild its walls.

While in exile the Hebrews had found it convenient to use the Aramaic (Syrian) style of writing and Aramaic speech. The speech was much like their own; the letters of the writing had been exactly like theirs in the beginning. But by the time of Nebuchadrezzar a century or so of hasty writing by Aramaic shop clerks had distorted the shapes of the letters. After the Hebrew return to Jerusalem the people did not revert to the letter shapes used before the exile. They kept on with the Aramaic forms, elaborating them into a temple-school script made with a reed pen having a broad nib. This, the "square Hebrew," as it is now called, was used for all religious writing.

Hebrew letter forms of today follow the square-Hebrew patterns of two thousand years ago. There are twenty-two letters, all for consonants. The writing runs from right to left. And, strangely enough, not a single one of today's symbols *has any resemblance to the original letter forms of Phoenician days,* as you can see by comparing the letter forms below.

The absence of vowel letters in the Hebrew manner of writing was originally of no importance. But eventually the meaning of certain words in the Hebrew Scriptures came to be in doubt; there would be two words, perhaps, with the same consonants but different vowels. A punctuation plan of dots and little dashes placed above or below the consonant letters was

From early Aramaic (top) to square Hebrew (bottom)

developed. This indicated the vowels and also showed word-tone and emphasis in Scripture reading.

Hebrews use their square-letter script today for Yiddish, a language with a mixture of German and Hebrew words as the main vocabulary. In such writing, four of the twenty-two letters are used for vowels.

Arabic Writing

The Arabic alphabet is, after the Latin, the most widely used of all alphabets. From certain Malay islands off the coast of Asia, on across two continents to Morocco on the Atlantic —that is the vast spread of Arabic script. The letter forms of this writing, like those of the Hebrews, go back for a begin-

Arabic	Transliteration	English word
الكيميا	al-kīmīa	alchemy
الكحل	al-koh'l	alcohol
الجبر	al-jebr	algebra
القبة	al-qobbah	alcove
القلى	al-qalīy	alkali
الانبيق	al-anbīq	alembic
الخوارزمي	al-Khowārazmī	algorism

The al, appearing in the seven interesting Arabic words that are given, had the meaning of "the." Thus the fourth word meant "the cave." In the English words reaching us through the Spanish the al has been blended into the rest of the word. So "the cave" is "alcove."

ning to the ancient alphabet of the Phoenicians. As in Hebrew writing, there had been a period of letter-form change, followed by a rigidity of letter shape that came from use in religious writings. But with the Arabians the period of change lasted half a thousand years longer than with the Hebrews. And by that time the swinging curves of Arabic writing had lost all resemblance to any other manner of writing found in either the ancient or the modern world.

Up to the year that Mohammed died (632 A.D.), Arabic writing was unknown beyond the borders of Arabia. By the close of the following century the green crescent of the followers of Mohammed had been carried by victorious Moslem armies to China in the east and Spain and Morocco in the west, and Moslem empires were established on three continents. The religion so established used as its sacred Scriptures the *Qur'an*, a book compiled by Mohammed himself. It was the Arabic manner of writing in the *Qur'an* (or Koran, as we of the West write the word) which became the writing standard for the Moslem world.

The Arabic alphabet has twenty-eight letters—the ancient list of twenty-two with six additional consonants. The extras

Greetings from Prince Houssain.

A copy of a message from Prince Houssain to merchants visiting Baghdad. It is of course written from right to left. So is my translation. Look at it in a mirror if you cannot decipher it.

GREEK

Α	α	alpha	a
Β	β	beta	b
Γ	γ	gamma	g
Δ	δ	delta	d
Ε	ε	epsilon	ĕ
Ζ	ζ	zeta	z
Η	η	eta	ē
Θ	θ	theta	th
Ι	ι	iota	i
Κ	κ	kappa	k
Λ	λ	lambda	l
Μ	μ	mu	m
Ν	ν	nu	n
Ξ	ξ	xi	x
Ο	ο	omicron	ŏ
Π	π	pi	p
Ρ	ρ	rho	r
Σ	ς σ	sigma	s
Τ	τ	tau	t
Υ	υ	upsilon	ū
Φ	φ	phi	ph
Χ	χ	chi	kh
Ψ	ψ	psi	ps
Ω	ω	omega	ō

are for the finer shades of sound of the spoken language. Three of these are described as being "lisping modifications," and the other three as "guttural modifications." In present-day Arabic, dots and small accent marks indicate the nature of the vowel that follows the marked consonant. All writing is from right to left, in Phoenician style. "In spite of its puzzling appearance to the novice, Arabic writing is comparatively easy to decipher." That is the comment of a friend of mine recently returned from Iraq.

The Modern Greek Alphabet

The alphabet in use in modern Greece may be considered the oldest in the world. Its capital-letter forms are those of Athens of over two thousand years ago. No addition or omission has been made. In modern Greek literature the spellings are also those of ancient Greece—though word pronunciations have changed somewhat with the passing centuries.

The Greek minuscule, or small-letter, forms are only about

half as old as the others; they came into
use among the book scribes about the year
800. And we may wonder whether Alcuin
got his idea for the Latin minuscules from
having seen the Greek letters, or whether
the Greeks got the idea from him. For
both groups it was the shortage of parchment that made the use of small-sized
letters so important. Perhaps the most surprising thing about the Greek minuscule
forms was the confusing difference in appearance between them and the capitals.
Almost half of them look as if they were
for some strangely different alphabet, as
you can tell by running down the list.

The Russian Alphabet

While the Greeks are the only people
using their ancient alphabet, the Rus-
sians, Serbs, and Bulgarians have alphabets based upon the Greek. These people
have a Slavonic form of language, with
many consonant-letter sounds not appearing in the Greek. A special alphabet, devised in the year 861, put in additional
letters for these sounds. The task of
alphabet-building had been turned over
to two brothers sent out as missionaries to
the Slavs from the headquarters of the Greek Catholic Church

RUSSIAN

А	а	a
Б	б	b
В	в	v
Г	г	g
Д	д	d
Е	е	e
Ж	ж	zh
З	з	z
И	и	i
Й	й	ǐ
К	к	k
Л	л	l
М	м	m
Н	н	n
О	о	o
П	п	p
Р	р	r
С	с	s
Т	т	t
У	у	u
Ф	ф	f
Х	х	kh
Ц	ц	ts
Ч	ч	ch
Ш	ш	sh
Щ	щ	shch
Ь	ь	'
Ы	ы	y
Ъ	ъ	'
Э	э	e
Ю	ю	yu
Я	я	ya

at Constantinople. The alphabet was needed so that the Bible might be translated into Slavic. The brothers were Greeks who had been raised in the city of Salonika and were able to speak the Slav tongue fluently. Cyril, the more learned and literary, handled the problem by using Greek letters as far as possible; special letters were devised for the rest. New names were given to all the letters, each being called by the name of some object starting with that sound. (This part of the plan was like the Runic naming scheme.) The one with the B sound was called *buki*, "beech-tree," that with the D sound was *dobro*, "oak," and so on.

Eleven centuries have passed since Cyril's time. Word sounds changed somewhat in that time among the Slavs as with other people. The full list of forty-eight symbols in the old list was not needed. In 1918 Russia adopted an official revision in which a third of the letters were either dropped or merged into other letters of somewhat similar sounds. The Serbs and Bulgarians still keep the longer list.

The remaining Slavonic people of Europe, the Slovenes, Croats, Slovaks, Poles, Wends, and Lusatians, were Christianized not from Constantinople but from Rome. Roman missionaries used the Latin alphabet in their translations of the Bible into Slavonic words. To handle the additional sounds not found among the Latin, the translators used letter combinations for some, added accent marks for the letters C, S, and Z, for others. This way of getting around the difficulty of fitting an old alphabet to some new language form encouraged pronunciation troubles, as in family names of Poles and Slovaks. But it held down the number of letter symbols.

Epilogue

The writing of the Chinese is the only ancient non-alphabetic system in extensive use. I am assured that the reason for this apparent lack of advance lies in the Chinese language. One feature of its manner of speech is the emphasis upon pitch, the tone in which a word is spoken being as important as the vowel sounds would be in our words.

In conclusion, just a comment.

Perhaps you may have felt, as I have, that the world may be entering a new era in the art of communication. For three thousand years the producer of the written word has tried out his way. But the intonation, the shades of meaning that a speaker could add are missing from the printed page—unless we, the readers, can supply them from our own thinking. There are in use today mechanical devices by which spoken words may be temporarily imprisoned. A message sent by mail may contain within its wrappings something quite different from the age-old markings of ink upon paper. It may contain the record of the voice carried upon plastic, tape, or wire. Perhaps in a generation or so the communication methods of the world may be affected. Then, perhaps, the libraries will be stored with voice records rather than with books.

Bibliography

It is customary in a book of this kind to list some references for extra reading. Many books have been written on the origin of the alphabet. Most of these are now obsolete. New archaeological discoveries have a way of upsetting old interpretations. Unfortunately the accounts of the results at Gebal and Ugarit are not available in English translations of the original reports. The best book for the reader is *The Alphabet* by David Diringer (New York: Philosophical Society, 1948). This is an expensive book, erudite, very comprehensive. The first chapter of Part Two deals with the development of alphabetic writing.

Reference books on hand-lettering are more available. City, school, and college libraries have them on the shelves. Among the best references for general reading are the following.

The Book by D. C. McMurtrie (New York: Covici, Friede, 1937). This is a well-told story of printing and bookmaking. The first 212 pages carry the story of writing up through the times of the early printers.

In Quest of the Perfect Book by W. D. Orcutt (Boston: Little, Brown & Company, 1926). Chapter 6 gives full-page reproductions of printing by Gutenberg, Jenson, and Aldus, as well as a manuscript page from Alcuin's Bible.

A good magazine article on the excavation of ancient Ugarit is "New Alphabet of the Ancients is Unearthed" by F. A. Schaeffer in the *National Geographic Magazine* for October 1930, pages 477–516. For examples of cuneiform writing, see "Darius Carved History on Ageless Rock" by George G. Cameron in the *National Geographic Magazine* for December 1950, pages 825–844.

The *Encyclopaedia Britannica* has many articles that make good reading. The following are excellent: Runes; Calligraphy, the art of fine writing; Jebeil, a name for ancient Gebal; Abacus; Numerals. The *Encyclopedia Americana* gives a good but brief treatment of Sequoyah, the genius of the Cherokees.

Index